May the messages and teachings within my father's sermons provide you with the same inspiration, mindfulness and joy as they have for me upon gathering these sermons together for this book.

Michael L. Thompson

!!!

Roger L. Thompson was ordained at First Lutheran Church in Cincinnati, Ohio on May 18, 1960.

On December 28, 2014, Roger Thompson preached his final sermon as Pastor of Trinity Lutheran Church in Willard, Ohio.

Contents

The People Who Ministered to Him 1
I Was There Too 9
The White Christian and His Negro Neighbor 17
Reply to Threats on My Life 27
The Sin Beyond Forgiveness 33
Born Anew—Daily 43
God's Use of Church Buildings 49
Resurrection...A Present Reality 55
Let Us Return to Bethlehem 59
The Good News in a Single Sentence 65
Where Do We Go from Here? 71
Oh, What a Relief It Is! 75
Already Forgiven—Even Before Asking 81
And They Placed a Crown of Thorns on His Head 87
It Is No Longer I Who Live But Christ Who Lives Within Me 93
Appendix 101

April 8, 1962

The People Who Ministered to Him

After spending five weeks of preaching about the people who were in some way or another, responsible for the death of Jesus, we now turn to the story of those people who were kind to Him and who tried to help Him in His hours of passion. Let us then take a few minutes to trace these familiar steps that lead from the Judgement Hall of Pilate to the cruel Cross of Calvary—those steps that were full of pain and suffering, and yet occasionally marked by a kind and ministering hand.

"Ibis Ad Crucem." Those were the words uttered by Pontius Pilate as he sentenced our Lord to the Cross. It was a verdict of death by crucifixion, the most cruel and dreaded form of death in all the ancient world, a death reserved only for slaves and criminals. Now, this method of execution had originated in the land of Persia, a land where it was believed that the earth was sacred and should never be defiled with the body of a criminal or an evil-doer. It was the land therefore where the people placed those to be executed high upon crosses. From Persia, crucifixion moved on to Carthage in North Africa…and from there it came to Rome, even though the Romans never used it on their own people.

Now after the sentence of crucifixion had been given, it was the custom of the Romans to then take the prisoner and give him a good scourging. And believe me it was a terrible torture. In fact, many of the condemned actually died of scourging before they even reached the cross. Of course, we know that Jesus survived the scourging that he received and was, therefore, led to the Cross.

Now, it was also the custom that the condemned man should carry his own Cross to the place of crucifixion. In many pictures we see Jesus carrying the WHOLE Cross, but really it was the cross-beam that he carried, because the upright was usually already waiting at the scene of the crucifixion. And yet after a torturous beating, even a cross-beam was very heavy. In front of Jesus, as He carried His Cross, there walked one of the Roman soldiers with a sign on which was written the crime for which he was going to die. A sign that was later to be nailed to the top of His Cross, a sign that had this written on it, "Jesus of Nazareth, King of the Jews."

And then, to make the trip to the Cross even more agonizing, it was the custom to lead the condemned down as many streets as possible, thus taking not the shortest, but the longest way to the Cross. It seems that there was a two-fold purpose behind this. First, so that many people as possible might see it, and thereby realize that "crime doesn't pay." And secondly, so that if anyone could bear witness to the innocence of the condemned man, they might step forward and do so—in which case of course, the procession was halted, and the case was retried.

Now as I said before, Jesus had begun to carry His own cross, but because of the weight of it, plus His own lack of strength from the beating He had taken, He found that He could carry it no further. It was at this time that Simon of Cyrene was called into action. One Dr. Sangster put it in these words, "The soldiers caught hold of Simon and made him carry the cross of Jesus. I don't suppose that he wanted to. I'd imagine that Simon felt as you or I would have felt...that we just didn't want to get involved...that we'd just as soon keep out of the whole mess. But after he was forced into service, and saw that piteous, bloodstained figure, and the unearthly look of the Son of God, don't you think that some pity must have stirred in his heart?" Well, all that I can personally say is that regardless of the feelings that Simon might have had when he carried Jesus' Cross, he did do it, and there certainly isn't any record of his rebelling against it. And so, then, this man, Simon of Cyrene was the very first to offer a "ministering" hand to our Lord Jesus.

Now, the place to which they took him was called the "Place of the Skull," in Hebrew "Golgotha," and in Latin "Calvary." When they finally reached the place of crucifixion, the cross was laid flat on the ground...Jesus upon it...His hands nailed to it...His feet loosely bound but not nailed...and between his legs was placed a ledge of wood so that the weight of his body would not pull him from the cross. The cross was then lifted upright and sat in its socket. Now, the cross really wasn't very tall as we picture it today. In fact, it was really shaped more like a "T," having no top piece at all.

Well then, it was just at this moment that the second kind

thing was done to our Lord Jesus, even though He actually refused the offer. It seems that there was a kind of "Guild" in Jerusalem, made up of women who in order to help the many people crucified in those days, came to every crucifixion and gave the condemned a drink of drugged wine to ease the terrible pain. Well as I said, the drink was offered to Jesus, but He refused it. Once again, in spite of the refusal, we can certainly see the merciful intention, and thus the second hand to minister onto our Lord in His dying hours.

Now, the third ministering hand came from the soldier who moistened Jesus' lips when He cried, "I thirst." Seven times our Lord spoke upon the Cross, but only once about His physical suffering. Once again, in the words of Dr. Sangster, "And then that rough soldier darted forward and moistened the lips of Jesus. Now say what you like about it," says Dr. Sangster "but it was kind—a spot a pity in the midst of hate." And so, the third to minister unto Jesus.

Of course, we can't forget either the little band of Jesus' followers who accompanied Him, even to the Cross…His mother Mary, John, Mary Magdalene, and Mary the mother of James to name just a few. Now, of course, they didn't directly minister to Jesus, but their very presence at the Cross must certainly have brought some comfort to Jesus, especially since He knew that they were risking their very lives by being there. For you see, it was a very dangerous thing to be an associate of a man considered dangerous enough to deserve the Cross. And remember, crucifixion was very shameful thing. And so, in a manner of speaking, those who were there with Him were, in a sense sharing His shame with Him.

And then the final person to "minister" to Jesus was the man about who we've already spoken, the "penitent thief." As I've already stated, this man was responsible for the last kind word ever spoken to our Lord Jesus Christ. In fact, I think we can say that the "penitent thief" was the first person to really realize the purpose and the power of Jesus' Cross and perhaps even the first person to give a vocal witness to it. I think we can truthfully say that the witness of the "penitent thief" was as relieving and comforting to Jesus as the Cross-bearing of Simon, and the lip-moistening of the centurion soldier.

My friends, there is a message in all of this for those of us who live today, but to see this message, we must first ask ourselves, "Is it possible for Jesus to still be ministered unto, this day and age?" Well perhaps, we've really never thought of it in this way, but isn't it true that there are still crosses to carry for Jesus? Still risks of life and reputation to be taken for His name's sake? And, isn't it true that there exist, even today, physical needs as well as spiritual needs in our world? And what about the great need for testimonies and witnesses to the great power of Jesus cross? I don't think there's any question about it. In fact, I would say that everything that I've mentioned, should be a part of every Christian's life.

I think Jesus made it very clear when He said that "If any man would come after me, let him deny himself and take up his cross and follow me." And yet as I said last Sunday, there are many different kinds of crosses that people bear, and certainly not all of them bring honor and glory to Christ. For instance, crosses that create resentment towards God, or self-pity for oneself, certainly aren't carried in the name of Christ. But crosses that help others see the faith and the confidence that the bearer still has in his God, these are crosses the truly "minister" unto Jesus.

But what about this "risking of our reputation and life for the sake of Christ"? Well the words of Jesus were "for whosoever would save his life will lose it, and whoever loses his life for my sake will find it." Now, every day Christians are called upon to either do something or not do something with the risk and danger that they might be "made fun of" or lose out on some worldly gain. It seems as if this is the constant temptation of our children and young people today...whether to do something that they know to be wrong or risk the chance of someone calling them "chicken" or "yellow." Of course, with us adults, it's our pride and our desire to get-ahead in the world that keeps us away from the Cross. In other words, because of our fear of being associated with the man named Jesus.

And what about the physical needs of Jesus? Remember these words, "Lord, when did we see thee hungry and feed thee, or thirsty and give thee something to drink" and "Truly, I say to you, as you did it to one of the least of these, my brethren, you did it to me."

Perhaps we should remember these words when, as Christians, we are encouraged to help the needy in foreign countries, and even right here at our own back-door. For certainly, to feed and clothes those in need is the same as to minister unto our "thirsting" Lord.

And was the penitent thief meant to be the only one to ever give witness to the purpose and the power of Jesus' Cross? You'd certainly believe so the way so many Christians keep their faith and belief to themselves, never once telling another person what Jesus means to them. Sometimes I wonder if we Christians realize that our "ministering" unto Jesus also includes this ministry of witness and testimony. The same ministry, referred to by Christ Himself when He said, "Go therefore and make disciples of all nations."

I had asked the question, "Is it possible for Jesus to still be ministered unto, in this day and age?" Well, what do you think? When Jesus says, "If you do it unto the least of them my brethren, you do it unto me" doesn't this really show that time doesn't make any difference whatsoever in our ministering unto Jesus? Doesn't it show that our "ministering" unto Jesus today is really no different from those who "ministered unto Him" when He was on the Cross?

My friends who will you be? Simon of Cyrene? The "followers" at the Cross? The Roman soldier? Or the penitent thief? Or perhaps all of those who "ministered unto Jesus." Really, I say, there is no choice.... for you see the calling of a Christian is to be all of these.

Amen

April 7, 1966 (Maundy Thursday)

I Was There Too

The Fall of Rome...The death of Joan of Arc...The nailing of Luther's 95 Theses to the door of Wittenberg Church...The Battle at Gettysburg. Not one of us was present when these great events took place. Outside of their historical interest and significance, they probably matter very little to most of us. This is the way that it is with events in history which happened before our time—and yet, my friends there was one event which took place in the history of Man—57 generations ago, to be exact, an event which is for some people just as significant today as it was the very day it happened. That event, of course, was the crucifixion of Jesus Christ. Yes, for some people, that occurrence is just as meaningful and just as relevant as if it had happened only last Friday. But for a great many others, because it really took place almost a million Fridays ago, it seems quite insignificant and irrelevant.

Now, most of these latter persons do not, of course, doubt or disbelieve that the crucifixion actually took place, but rather what they do question is, "Did it happen for ME? How can I feel that the Cross is not just an historical act of the past, but how can I begin to feel that it is something that is personal and relevant for me today as well?" Perhaps, what they are really asking is, "How can I get ME into the crucifixion?" This I must say is one of the greatest problems facing the Christian Church today—and that is that the Cross has become a very impersonal thing for a great many people in our present day and age. And believe me, they are not all on the outside of the Church either. There are a great many people who claim the name of Christian who believe in their minds that Christ died on the Cross, but who have tremendous difficulties believing in their hearts that He died for them.

Here, this evening, I would like to consider with you FOUR things that I feel a person must feel and believe before the Crucifixion of Christ can ever become a relevant personal part of your life and mine.

The very first thing that we must possess is a feeling of need for a Savior. Now, this may sound like rather a simple statement, but you'd be surprised how many people there are who do not at all think of themselves as being "sin-sick." Oh, a little bad—we're all a wee-bit sinful, but "sin-sick"? Diseased with badness? Me? Yes, you and me and every man—but not every man realizes that he is. My friends, just as a person will not normally go to the hospital for an operation unless his doctor can convince him that he is sick enough to warrant or need the surgery—so a man will not go the Cross and seek healing from it unless he is convinced that he is a "sin-sick" sinner. And this is the only way that Jesus and His Cross can ever become a personal-relevant thing for us—when we realize and feel very deeply that we are in great need of forgiveness and cleansing. Yes, the Cross is irrelevant and impersonal for a lot of people today simply because they are not able to confess like St. Peter did, "Lord, depart from me, for I am a sinful man." It is not enough, I say, to simply make a confession with your lips as you we do often at our worship services, but rather it must also be felt in the depth of our hearts. We must feel by nature sinful and unclean. We must really believe that we are unworthy sinners who have grievously offended God, and who have merited only his wrath and condemnation. These feelings must be personal, and they must be felt.

The first step then to the Cross is this feeling of need for Jesus as our very own personal Savior. It is a realization that without Christ we would be lost—left alone to die of "disease" that would eventually send us into an eternity of despair and nothingness. One Sir James Simpson, a famed Scottish surgeon, discovered this need for a personal Savior and stated thus when he said in answer to a question about his greatest discovery, "My greatest discovery is that I am a very great sinner—and that Jesus is a very great Savior." I wonder, can you and I say as much?

The second step, then in making the Crucifixion of Jesus more meaningful and personal to us is that of believing that the Cross was a very necessary thing. Perhaps, you're asking, "Well, who would doubt it?" But you'd be surprised how many people there are who ask, "Well couldn't God have some other way of dealing with the sin of man without the Cross? After all, God can do anything can't he?" And, you see, behind all of these questions is the implication that the Crucifixion might have been by-passed had God simply declared us forgiven and let it go at that.

The fact is, my friends, that there is one thing that God cannot do—yes, I say, there is one thing our God controls—and that is that he cannot contradict his own divine nature by tolerating sin or by making light of it. To do so would be a denial of the very nature of God. In other words, because sin is such a terrible offense and insult to holiness of God, the divine nature of God will not permit or allow him to simply pass-over sin lightly—as we would, at many times, like for him to do so. No, my friends, the word of God is quite clear at this point—that sin demands a punishment. It demands a price—a price that someone has to pay. And the tragedy of humanity, you see, is that the price is far too great for any man to pay for himself. The debt is too great. The infection—the disease—is too deep and far-spread. And this simply, but plainly, means that man without the Cross is lost to sin—a slave to that which is completely opposite to God Himself.

Here again then, is where the Crucifixion of Christ can become a personal, meaningful relevant thing for you and me today—for we too need someone to pay our debt for us—to break the of sin in our life—and to open the doors of the Kingdom of God for us. We can't do it ourselves—and this then, you see, is what makes the Cross a necessity—both the seriousness of our sin and the Holiness of God. It is as simple as this—the Cross was necessary, you see, because God cannot lightly pass-over sin—and also, because there was a debt to be cancelled and a power to be defeated. This meant that there had to be a battle—a victory—a sacrifice—a ransom paid—and even though it is extremely difficult for some of us to believe this—God knew that He was the only One Who could achieve these things. God in Christ had to do for us what was impossible for us to do for ourselves. To believe this my friends, to really believe it, deep down—is to make the Crucifixion of Christ a very relevant thing for this day and every day.

We come, now, to the third step—a step that is very closely related to the first that was mentioned. For in order for the Cross of Jesus to really mean something to us, we must not only feel the need for its benefits—and sincerely want them—but we must also be convinced in our hearts and minds that these benefits are still available to us today. In other words, the length of time between 1969 and when the Crucifixion actually happened is very great—and, believe me, sometimes it's quite difficult for a person to really feel that it was done for him personally and individually. And I must admit to you that have been times when this has been a problem for me too—to feel that what Jesus did 2000 years ago was actually for me—today.

But when you really begin to think about it seriously—aren't there really a great many things from which you and I benefit today that were originated many, many years before we were even born? What about the discoveries in medicine and science? For instance, take the discovery of anesthetics—or the pasteurization of milk? Or take the establishment of our country, and all of its democratic rights and privileges? Certainly, it isn't too difficult to see how a thing that was done before we were even born can, in fact, benefit us and be available to us even today in 1969? As an anonymous poet once put it, "Under an Eastern sky, Amid a rabble cry, A man went forth to die, For me." That is the third feeling that we must have if the Crucifixion of Christ is to be relevant and significant for us today.

We come then, to the fourth and final step in our attempt to make the Cross a personal matter in our lives. We have just seen how the benefits of the Cross can be ours even today—and now we must come to see that these benefits can actually become our possession even if we don't fully understand or comprehend how God made all of this possible. You know, we can sometimes get so wound up in the mechanics of the Cross—that is, in the "theological" meaning of it—that we fail to see that it is the Cross itself which saves us, and not our understanding of it.

My friends, I know of a good many Christians who can't even come close to giving you a good theological explanation of the Crucifixion—but they can say, "I believe with all of my heart that Jesus suffered and died on a cross, and that he did it for me." You see, this is the way that it is with the Cross of Jesus. We may not have the ability to grasp all of its meaning—but still the benefits can come to use if we feel the need for them and ask for them. Thank goodness, I say, that our salvation does not rest upon our intellectual understanding and comprehension of all that God has done for us in Christ through the Cross. If it did, many of us would surely be lost, wouldn't we?

In conclusion then, I would like to impress upon you this one final thought. I have been trying to show you this evening in four simple steps, how the Crucifixion of Christ can become a more meaningful, personal, and relevant thing for you and me today—in 1969. First, I said by feeling a deep need for a Savior from our sins. Secondly by believing that the Cross was really necessary in that God had to do something for us that was utterly impossible for us to do for ourselves. And thirdly, that the benefits of the Cross are still just as available today as they were to the people of Jesus' own day. And finally, that the benefits of the Cross are available to us even if we can't fully understand how God went about this business of saving of our souls.

But there remains still one more important factor in making the Crucifixion of Jesus relevant for us today—perhaps, the most important factor of all—and that is simply this—that it was just as much our sin today, that placed Jesus on His Cross as it was the sin of those who were directly responsible for the foul deed of Calvary. This, my friends, we must believe, and feel in the depth of our hearts—and there is no better way to impress this upon minds and hearts than by ending with this little story, possibly true, but probably a legend. A Story of the thief Barabbas, who as you know, should have died on the Cross that Jesus died on, but was chosen by the people to be released instead of Jesus. Well, the story goes that Barabbas, when he realized that he was free—rushed into the local tavern, and there became drunk in the wild excited joy of his friends. Later on that day, as he was wandering home in a drunken stupor, he passed by the hill upon which Jesus was crucified—and as he did so, something seemed to draw him up the hill. Some irresistible force seemed to be carrying him to the very foot of the Cross in the middle. Slowly he looked upward until his eyes fell on the crucified body of our precious Savior—and suddenly, Barabbas was shocked into a state of soberness—a wild explosive fire broke loose within his heart—and flinging his arms across his eyes, he cried out, "My God, My God, that's MY cross he's dying on."

Amen.

June 4, 1967

The White Christian and His Negro Neighbor

Background notes: From my South Haven, Indiana experience when I participated in a "rural summer vacation" program sponsored by Valparaiso University and Porter County Ministerial Association. This is the first of two sermons preached at Our Savior Church of which I was the Pastor. And two newspaper articles related the event (see Appendix). This is the sermon preached which caused the South Haven reaction to our hosting a boy named Tony in our home.

In many all-white communities, a sermon such as the one that I shall preach this morning would probably result in the loss of several members and a fair number of prospective members as well. And yet only time will show the results of my sermon on this congregation, but if this particular congregation in any way reflects the great amount of racial prejudice which is generally found in Porter County, then I would image that I'm not going to be a very popular pastor around here after this morning. And yet, these are the things which I feel that I must risk if I am to be true to my own inner convictions and to what seems to me to be the testimony of God's Holy Word. Now you can say and feel what you like about me, but in the end, your opinion and feelings must also come under the judgement of God and His Word.

Racial prejudice you know is grounded in ignorance. People who have prejudice toward Negroes are simply feeling instead of thinking. In other words, they're reacting emotionally rather than intellectually. You know I have spent these past several weeks reading all of the literature that I could find pertaining to this "racial" issue and when I sat down at my desk to write this sermon, I discovered that there were far more facts that I would like to present than there is time to do so. And so, I cannot possibly say all that needs to be said in this one sermon, I can only hope that those of you who have the true spirit of Christ within you will be so inspired as to seek more knowledge and understanding on your own. I would like to think that one of the results of this sermon—one of the good results—would be the desire for special discussion groups in our congregation on this very problem—the relationship of the White Christian with his Negro Neighbor.

Therefore, I have carefully selected the areas that I would like to cover this morning. First, I would like to confront you with the Biblical witness and then, I would like for you to see what the Christian Church has done and said with respect to the Negro. And finally, I would like to share with you not only my own personal feelings and actions on behalf of our Negro brothers, but also those of our Lutheran Church in America and those of the Porter County Ministerial Association of which I am a part.

Now, I know that some people have heard that the Bible itself advocates an inferior position to the Negro race, but people who believe this are either so greatly prejudiced from the start that they use the Bible by twisting it to agree with their own feelings—or else they are simply Biblically illiterate. The fact is that the Bible through the teaching of Christ and His apostles condemns prejudice of all sorts. Now I can't begin to quote the passages which should make every one of us ashamed that we wouldn't want a Negro family to live next door to us simply on the basis of the fact that they were Negroes. Even Jesus himself was condemned by His disciples for simply talking to a Samaritan. For you see, the Jews hated Samaritans because they were of a mixed race and not of pure Jewish stock like the other Jews. And yet to Jesus every living human being—regardless of his color, his moral standards, or anything else—was a person to be loved and with whom he was willing to dine, socialize, and even live. My friends, by His life, by His example, Christ is telling us that it is wrong—that it is evil to segregate the races.

As one of my seminary professors, Dr. T.A. Kantonen put it, "In light of Jesus' basic teaching on human relations, it is impossible for us to escape the fact that that the whole pattern of racial discrimination and segregation is seen as an unutterable offense against God. And it is should be clear," he said, "that Christians who defend segregation cannot do so as Christians" and that they can only do so "in direct conflict with the mind of Christ."

Let me try to explain it this way. In last week's Epistle Lesson, in the first letter of St. John it is written, "He who does not love his brother whom he has seen, cannot love God whom he has not seen." And yet I ask you, how can love you a "brother" when you don't even allow yourself to associate with him—when you refuse to relate to him as a real neighbor. In other words, when you won't allow him to live within your community? How can you love someone at a distance—at arm's length? My friends, our unwillingness to live with Negroes simply on the basis of the fact that are Negroes—this unwillingness—must fall under the judgement of God's Word—"He who does not love his brother whom he has seen, cannot love God whom he has not seen."

Of course, there are Negroes who would not make the kind of neighbor that we might want as a neighbor, but there are a number of white people here in South Haven whom I wouldn't particularly want as neighbors either. And of course, there are some Negroes who have low moral standards, but not all of them—and when you take a good hard look at what's been going on here in South Haven and in other white communities across the nation, I don't think that we are in any position to point the finger at Negroes' moral standards. And sure, there are some Negroes who don't take care of their property but look around here. Overall, there are some Negroes that I have known in my life that I would much rather live next to than some of the whites right here in our own community. And I really mean it.

Now you see it's one thing to say that we wouldn't want to live next door to someone because of this particular reason or that, but to simply say we don't live next door to Negroes because they are Negroes—I say this prejudice, racial prejudice—and an offense against God. Actually, when we say that we don't want to live or associate with Negroes simply because they are Negroes and for no other reason, then we are saying that we do not consider them as equals with the white race. And this belief—that the white race is superior to the black race—is a complete contradiction of the Holy Scriptures. I defy anyone to show me in the Bible where it says that God loves one race more than another—or that that He created one race inferior to the others. Now many white Christians, I am afraid, actually believe that the Negro is an inferior human being. And really, that is all the average Negro wants—to be treated as an equal—as a human being—as a person.

I'm sure that some of you have heard of Malcom Boyd, the Episcopal priest who wrote the book, "Are You Running with Me Jesus?" Well, in another of his books entitled, "The Hunger, the Thirst" he says that that this is precisely what the racial struggle is all about—the struggle of a race of people who have been treated for hundreds of years as anything but truly human—their struggle to be truly human beings. One of Father Boyd's prayers reads like this (from pages 51-52 in "Are You Running With Me Jesus"):

> *Yes, what does God say about us? Does He see the color that we see? Does the color of a man's skin make a difference to God? Did Christ only die for the white man? Will Heaven be segregated? Will we be able to keep our sons and daughters from socializing with Negroes in God's external Kingdom? And, which would be most disturbing to God—that our children married a white atheist or a Negro Christian? Yes, what does God think? And how can you and I call ourselves Christians and not care what God thinks?*

Now, you would think that with this Biblical under-girding, the Church would have been one of the first to support the Negro in his struggle for equal rights, but the fact of the matter is that the Church has been of the last forces to come to the aid of the Negro. In fact, in one of the books that I read, the author made the indictment that the Church has actually perpetuated racial prejudice and discrimination in the years gone by. As the author, Kyle Haseld puts it, "The major sin of the white Christian church has been not merely its passive default in the field of interracial relations, but even more, its direct, positive, and sometime malicious contribution to the race-caste system in America." As he goes on to say, "The struggle of the American Negro toward freedom and fullness would have been hard enough with the help of the church but that, in tragic fact, the struggle had to be waged by the Negro often without the concern of the white church and sometimes against its cold and resolute opposition."

A white active Lutheran church member was heard to say, "Well, I might have to eat with the Negro, sit next to him on the bus or at a theatre. I might even have to live near to one, but thank God, I've still got my church." This was actually said and tragically, it's a simple indication of the fact that the Church has, in the past, done almost next to nothing to help the Negro, and has, in fact, in many, many cases been responsible for keeping the Negro "in his place"—in his "inferior" place—in his less than "human" place. As Dr. Gordon W. Allport, Professor of Psychology at Harvard University has put it, "On the average, the members of the Christian churches are more prejudiced and bigoted than the non-church members."

Now, I would like to think that there is a change taking place in the church today. I know that a good number of pastors have begun to speak-out and act on behalf of their Negro brothers. Almost all of the major denominations in America have taken a very firm stand on this racial matter. Our own LCA included. Now, I don't think that I need to state in detail what our church has said on this issue—for you can read it yourself in one of the copies that I have placed on the table in the narthex. And, for those of you who would like to be better informed on this whole thing, you will find other materials there as well that can be borrowed for your reading.

In fact, if any of you would like to think and feel as a Christian in this whole thing of treating the Negro like a real human-being "brother" in Christ, then I invite you to come out to the church tonight at 7pm when we will have the privilege of discussing these problems with some of our Negro brothers themselves. A few Negro members from our church in Gary—Calvary Lutheran Church—will be here with their pastor, Pastor John Johnson. And even though I already know of a few people who do intend to come, I have a strange feeling that most of you will probably not care enough to come, or else you simply won't come as a way of showing your displeasure for what I have said here this morning. I sincerely hope that you prove me wrong. This is one time that I hope I am wrong. 7PM here at the church.

Finally, I would like to share with you some of the happenings that are taking place in the Porter County Ministerial Association of which I am part. Recently through this Association, a Human Relations Council was established in Porter County principally for the purpose of preparing the people of Porter County for what is to, mentally, come—integration. And even before this was done the Ministerial Association issued a statement which read, in part, "To this end we desire to call upon our citizens and especially the members of our congregation to make known their acceptance of, and their desire to help implement, the right of all persons to secure a home within their financial ability, regardless of race, creed, or national background." And I, for one signed my name to this statement.

In fact, in order to help my children to better understand that a person with black skin is just as human as they are, my wife and I have decided to participate this summer in a program that is being sponsored by the Immanuel Lutheran Church in Valparaiso—a program called "The Rural Summer Vacation Program"—and this is a program in which my wife and I shall have a Negro child living in our home for two weeks, beginning June 24th. Now, a few people who have come to know about this have asked us, "Well why do you want to do this—what good will it accomplish?" Well, for one thing, as I said before, it'll help my child to know that a Negro is not really so different—as different as the white race in general pictures him—and how on earth are our children going to realize that people of other races are just as human as they are, unless they come into personal contact with them? This is exactly why so many of us have the prejudice that we do—simply because we have never really gotten to know a Negro on a friendship basis. I for one, want my child to have this opportunity. And I'm convinced that if more white children did have this opportunity—the next generation of adults would be able to live together in more peace and harmony than we are living in. But it isn't only for my children that we are doing this. It is for the Negro child himself. One of the stated purposes of this program is as follows:

"It is anticipated that these children will learn to know that there are, among the majority group, people who are truly human, people who care. And as a result of this experience of human concern, and with a continuing personal friendship that may develop between host and guest, hope may be enkindled in the hearts of these inner-city children—a hope that will fight off their frustration, bitterness, and hate—in order that when they have grown into manhood or womanhood they will take their God-intended responsible place in society and in the church."

Any, by the way, if anyone else would be interested in doing this very same thing, just let me know in the next few days. You know, I honestly think that we have a few people in our church who would do this if they didn't think they were alone in doing it. Perhaps this too is part of my reasons for participating in this program. To set an example, to give others courage. There are people, you know, who look to the pastor and his wife to "lead the way" so to speak.

In conclusion, I would like to say these few words. I have felt for some time that this congregation needed to know how their pastor felt about this Negro situation. Some of you have asked me, but most of you haven't and that's probably because you knew what I would say—you knew what I must say as a Christian—and, of course, this would only remind you of what you should say. A very good reason as I see it for avoiding the whole issue. But we're not going to avoid it any longer. In fact, I encourage any and all of you to share with me your own personal feelings on this matter. Perhaps we can help each other to understand and to grow.

Now I want to be understood that I don't intend to go off on some "crusade" over this whole thing. You won't hear me preaching about this every several weeks. After this sermon, I don't think that I need to. You know how I feel now, and you know how you should feel—and I don't think that you'll quickly forget it. I also want to be understood that I have no intention of aiding in any "forced integration" into our community, but on the other hand if I hear of a Negro family who have been refused residence in our community simply on the basis of their race—you can then bet your bottom dollar that my voice will be heard. And if we have any Negroes come to our church, which I personally think is bound to happen, I want it to be known that I will treat them like any other family. And if members of the church don't treat them the same, then my voice will be heard again.

My friends, there are always people who will say to their pastor, "Pastor, don't rock the boat. Don't get people upset. We don't want to lose any members or get anyone mad at us," but this just isn't me. I can't remain silent when my Christian convictions demand that I speak. As Sir Thomas Moore said in the play and movie, "A Man for All Seasons" just before he was to be killed, "It isn't difficult to keep alive, my friends, just don't make trouble, or if you make trouble, make the sort of trouble that's expected." And this, I feel is the kind of pastor that many of you would have me to be, but I'm afraid, my friends, that I cannot be this kind of pastor. Christ will not allow me, and I sincerely pray for the day when He will not allow you either to be this kind of person. Christians of the early Church were called "turners of the world upside down." I ask you…How can we claim the name of Christ and be any less?

Amen.

June 11, 1967

Reply to Threats on My Life

Last Sunday, as most you know, I preached a sermon on loving our neighbor—regardless of the color of that neighbor. I said nothing that Jesus himself did not say—with the exception of stating that in a couple of weeks, my wife and I would have a little Negro boy coming to live with us for two weeks. Now, I stated explicitly at that time why we are doing this—but since it seems that a number of people (some of our own included) wanted to believe something other than what I said—I would like to repeat my intention. First, I am doing this because I want to help a little boy who needs this kind of opportunity. I am simply doing what any Christian would consider doing. I am simply doing what Jesus said those who follow Him should do, "If you have done it unto the least of them, you have it done unto me." "Love your neighbor (that means all men) as you love yourself." "By this all men will know that you are my disciplines—if you have love for one another."

Last week's Epistle lesson read, "If anyone has the world's

goods and sees his brother in need, yet closes his heart against him, how does God's love abide in Him?" The week before that, the Epistle Lesson read, "He who does not love his brother whom he has seen, cannot love God whom he has seen." Why am I doing this? Surely not to force integration? And not to simply prove a point. And not to simply stir things up. Why I am doing this is simply because the love of Jesus Christ constrains me to do so. I repeat any true Christian would surely consider the same. Jesus said, "You shall know them by their fruits."

And now that you know why I am doing this thing for this Negro child—I want you to know how a couple of your fellow "neighbors" have reacted to it. Since last Sunday, I have received two threats on my life—with one nice friendly white neighbor actually threatening to put a bomb in our house. Now, if you think it'd be bad to have a Negro living next to you—how would you like to have one of these "nuts" living next door? Who says that the Negro cause the violence in our country? What bigots— what hypocrites we have in our community. And tragically, a few of these people even belong to our church.

Now, I must admit that when I first was informed about threats, I was very much alarmed. Nothing, like this had ever happened to me before. For a while, I was very much confused. I prayed about if for hours. I talked to Dr. Schultze from Valparaiso University, who's in charge of this program, and I discussed it with about 30 pastors and laymen at a conference that I attended this week up in Wisconsin—and I also discussed it with my wife. The Pastors and layman all felt that I must make the final decision, but that they were behind me all the way. Dr. Keyser from our own Synod office, and five other Synod and

LCA officers said that they, too, were behind me in what I was intending to do. I've given much thought to this whole thing. My wife and I have it discussed it thoroughly. We both felt that as far we were concerned, we were willing to risk it, but then we thought of the children. I told one of the pastors what my wife said at this point—what she said was, "Roger, even if it would endanger our children—what is more important—life or death?" And then, it came me, "Yes, what kind of life would I be saving my children for" and then I decided that I would rather have them dead, then to give-in to threats and have them live in a community where this kind of person went unchallenged and was allowed to get away with this kind of thinking. I wonder if you realize what it means to let people like go unchallenged? I've heard many white people around here say that the Negro wants to take away his rights by demanding some for himself—well what are these white people doing with by their threats, they try to tell us who we can have in our houses—and isn't this what these people are trying to do to me? They're trying to pick the people whom I can have in my house? Does anyone have this right? What if someone tried to tell you who you could invite to your home for two weeks? And what would we be saying to people like this if we yielded to them? Doesn't it make you just a little angry that we have people like this in South Haven?

Now, I know that many of you are going to try to convince me that I should yield to the threats—and not have the child. And I will—if you can find anything in the Bible to substantiate your convictions, because, you see, it's been the Word of God that has made me not yield. Personally, I believe that these threats will never be carried out. They were simply meant to intimidate. And yet, I also know that there are people in this world crazy enough to do such a thing. Therefore, I do intend to notify the authorities of this matter. I want these people to know that they can't bully people around.

And finally, let me say this. More than anything, there were thoughts that convinced me that I must do this thing. If I did yield, if I don't stand by my convictions—how could I ever stand in that pulpit from this time on—and tell you to put Christ first in your life. How could I ever preach on standing by your convictions—when I didn't myself? How could I ever preach on these words from the Bible, "If any man would come after me, let him deny himself and take up his Cross and follow me—for whoever would save his life will lose it—and whoever loses his life for my sake will save it." And how could we ever sing those hymns back around the 550's, 60's—such as 551 (2), 554 (4-5), 562 (3).

My friends, the Bible tells us that those who follow Christ will endure persecution and suffering—and even death. The early Christians are the greatest testimony to this fact. St. Paul said, "when we are persecuted, we must endure." St. Peter said in the Epistle lesson for today that "suffering is required" of those who would follow Christ—and he also said, "Who is there to harm you if you are zealous for what is right? But even if you do suffer for righteousness sake, you will be blessed. Therefore, have no fear of them," says Peter, "nor be troubled, but in your hearts reverence Christ as Lord."

I think that you can see, now, why I must do this thing. If I am to be a true to my faith a follower of Jesus Christ, I must stand by my convictions—I must stand up for what I think is His will—even if it means suffering and persecution. Now, I'm no martyr, I don't want to give up my life in this way, but I'm willing to do so. It just saddens me to think that so many of you are willing to yield to what your neighbors think rather than to stand by your own inner convictions. Please don't ask me to do it—I can't. I just hope that since it was you who took the original story out into the community that now, you'll take this story too—and I hope that you'll tell everyone just why I'm doing this—and tell them too what some of their fellow neighbors have done. Perhaps, it'll help this community to grow-up just a little bit. I ask you to pray for me—and whether or not you feel that I'm doing the right thing—I hope that you'll respect my right to do what I think is right. And perhaps through this whole thing—this congregation will grow just a little bit too.

In conclusion, I have only this to say—I would like to apologize to you—not for what I have said or done in the last week—but what I obviously haven't done before that time. I apologize to you for not helping you to know what it really means to be a Christian. I've failed an awful lot of you somewhere—and I'm sorry. Deeply sorry.

February 1, 1970

The Sin Beyond Forgiveness

My sermon this morning stems from a conversation that I had with Glenn Auxter last Sunday morning before Sunday School began. It seems that his adult class had been discussing that passage in the Bible which speaks of the unforgivable sin against the Holy Spirit, the one which reads, "For this reason I tell you: men can be forgiven any sin and any evil thing they say, but whoever says evil things against the Holy Spirit will not be forgiven. Anyone who says something against the Son of Man will be forgiven, but whoever says something against the Holy Spirit will not be forgiven—now or forever." Well, my friends the explanation that I gave briefly to Glenn last Sunday, I would like to share with you in more detail here this morning—and it's quite a fitting time, I think, to give you this message on "sin" and "forgiveness" since we'll be celebrating Holy Communion this morning.

Now maybe you yourself have never worried about committing a sin that is "unforgivable," but believe me, a lot of people have. In fact, I've had a few come to me about this in my ministry; people who have almost worried themselves to death that in some way they've sinned against the Holy Spirit and therefore, committed the "unforgivable sin."

Well, now, to get on with this matter, we're going to attempt to answer two primary questions: "How does a person sin against the Holy Spirit?" and "What makes this sin so unforgivable?" In other words, is there really a sin so great that the love of God in Jesus Christ cannot forgive it? Now, in order to fully understand just what Jesus meant when He made this statement (which by the way is recorded in the 12th chapter of Matthew, the 3rd chapter of Mark, and the 12th chapter of Luke), to really understand what Jesus meant, we've got to first understand what certain words from this statement actually meant back those days, for example, when Jesus was talking about the "Son of Man." Now, if you take this expression, "The Son of Man" in reference to Christ Himself, then it sounds like what He's saying is, "If you speak against me, that is, if you 'blaspheme' me, this is forgivable, but not when do so to the Holy Spirit."

Now, of course, at first glance, this doesn't seem to make much sense, especially since Jesus and the Holy Spirit are both "God," but then, when you examine closely what the Hebrew phrase "a son of man" actually meant, the whole thing begins to clear-up, for you see, when the Hebrews spoke of a "son of man" they simply meant "a man." In other words, "any man." For example, we say, "There is a man," but the Hebrews you see would say, "There is a son of man." And so then, it is felt by some commentators that what Jesus really meant was simply this "If any man speaks a word against "a man" that is, a fellow-man, this can be forgiven, but if anyone speaks a word against the Holy Spirit, it will not be forgiven."

To put it quite simply, Jesus, it would seem was not saying that it would be a graver sin to speak against the Holy Spirit than to speak against Him. For surely a sin against either is equally a sin against both, for both are of course the One God. Instead, you see Jesus was simply contrasting our sins against God with those against our fellow man, but of course, that still doesn't fully answer the questions, "what is or what are these unforgivable sins against the Holy Spirit" and what is it that makes them so unforgivable?"

Now to do this, we've got to take it in a progressive manner. First, this idea of "blaspheming" the Holy Spirit. Now, you see, we've got to understand what this meant to the people of Jesus' day. For example, the Jews saw the Holy Spirit of God having two main functions: Number 1, to bring God's truth to men and Number 2, to enable men to recognize and understand that truth once they saw and heard it. In other words, the people of Jesus' day felt that you had to have the Holy Spirit in order to receive and recognize God's truth in your life.

Now Jesus knew this, you see, but He also knew that the average Jew of His day had actually lost much of the Holy Spirit within him. Let me depict it this way. It's common knowledge, I think, that a person can lose any faculty that he has if he refuses or neglects to use it. For example, if a man lived in the dark long enough, he would eventually lose his faculty of sight, wouldn't he? Maybe some of you know what it's like to be in the hospital off your feet for a couple of weeks. You know you almost have to learn to walk all over again. And if any of you have ever gone back to school after being out for 10 or 15 years, you know what

I mean too by losing a certain faculty or ability by not having used it for a long time. For instance, there was a time when I could speak Spanish and German and write (quite well) both Latin and Greek, but not anymore, because you see I have failed to use them day-in and day-out. This happens to people who don't pray over a long period of time too, and also those who miss church for a few weeks in a row. You all know what I mean, I'm sure.

The point is simply this, Jesus saw in the Jews what they didn't see in themselves—that they had, for so long a time, been blind and deaf to the guidance of God through His Holy Spirit, insisting on their own way so long, that they had finally reached that point where they were no longer able to recognize God's truth of goodness even they saw it.

This, then you see, is how the Scribes and the Pharisees "blasphemed the Holy Spirit" by refusing to accept God's Divine Truth for their lives, and this you see, they had done in practice by saying the miraculous cures of Jesus were actually the work of the Devil, going so far as accusing Jesus of being "an ally of Satan" looking at the very power and grace of God itself and calling it "the work of the Devil." This, I say, was their "unforgivable" sin, their sin against the Holy Spirit, simply the sin of so often and so consistently refusing God's spiritual guidance that they couldn't even recognize it when it hit them smack in the face. And to think that this "unforgivable sin" was actually committed by people who, at least outwardly, were the most religious and most godly people of that day. Church people beware.

Yes, I say it could happen to us too and you know perhaps there's just something about being "godly" and "religious" at one point in your life that actually makes you susceptible to this sin of refusing God's will and grace at a later point in our life. Maybe it's complacency or self-satisfaction. Or maybe it's the attitude of the Scribes and Pharisees—"we've got it made," "we're in," "We're God's Chosen people," "We've been saved," "There's nothing to worry about." "I've been baptized; I'm confirmed; I go to church every Sunday, or almost." How easy it would be you see to become like the Scribes and the Pharisees, thinking ourselves to be very religious when, in fact, we were actually "blaspheming the Holy Spirit" without even knowing it. And that my friends is the most horrible part about this "unforgivable" sin, that a person can turn God off so unconsciously that over a long period of time, he is actually no longer able to receive and recognize God's will and grace for his life. It happened, my friend, to the Scribes and Pharisees—and it can also happen to us.

But now we finally come that question—"What is it that makes this sin so unforgivable?" "Won't God forgive a person any sin, even the sin of turning Him off?" Is there really a sin so bad that it's unforgivable? Well, the answer is YES—there is a sin so bad that it's "unforgivable," but it's not, you see, a matter of God not wanting to forgive, but rather not being able to forgive. And that, you see, is due to the nature of this "sin against the Holy Spirit."

Let me put it this way. I never really worry about the person who comes to me in anguish and says, "Pastor, I feel so guilty, I'm sure that I've committed the 'unforgivable' sin." And the reason, you see, why I don't worry about this person having committed this unforgivable sin is simply because the one person who cannot have committed this sin against God's Holy Spirit is the person who fears he or she has. For, you see, the very fact that a person worries about the possibility of having committed this sin (and is capable of feeling guilt), this, in itself, is proof that they have not done so. In other words, if you ever feel guilty of having committed this unforgivable sin, don't worry about it being "unforgivable," because, you see, it only becomes unforgivable when the "guilt" and "the shame" are absent.

The DANGER is, you see, that the feelings of "shame" and "guilt" in a person will begin to be replaced by feelings of spiritual pride and self-righteousness (like in the Scribes and Pharisees). I meet these people every day. As soon as I say something that reflects upon the sins in their life—immediately they begin telling me how "good" they are, how little "real bad" they've done in their life and how they're "just as good" as anyone else. And this, you see, is exactly the way that the Scribes and the Pharisees reacted to Jesus when He began to point out their sins to them. They became defensive and, in the process, they became more and more insensitive to their sins, and thereby, more and more incapable of true repentance.

Here, then, you see, we begin to find the answer to the question—"What makes this sin so unforgivable?" The answer is simply this. First, the sins against the Holy Spirit (the sin of blaspheming the Holy Spirit) is the sin of not wanting to be forgiven—of refusing God's forgiveness. And secondly, the reason why the Holy Spirit is "blasphemed" and God's forgiveness is refused—is simply because certain people, you see, reach the point in their life where they no longer feel the need to be forgiven. Just like the Scribes and Pharisees, they either feel that they don't really do enough bad things to feel guilty and therefore confess to God, or else they simply feel that the good in their life outweighs the bad, therefore excusing them from the need for God's forgiveness. And thirdly, this is why the person who thinks he or she has committed the unforgivable sin is usually the least likely to have done so, simply because the person who does commit the sin is almost always never aware of it.

Now I think that the most important thing that I can say at this time is simply this. The good news of Jesus Christ is that any sin can be forgiven with the exception, of course, of the sin of not wanting to be forgiven, or not feeling the need to be. Therefore, you see, the thing that makes this sin against the Holy Spirit so "unforgivable" is not that God won't forgive, but that He can't because the person won't let him. And you see, this is the way it is with God. God simply will not force his love and forgiveness on a person. They must want it. They must feel the need for it. Therefore, the only sin that is really unforgivable is the sin of refusing God's love and forgiveness—the same sin, you see, of which Jesus was condemning the Scribes and the Pharisees.

Believe me, my friends—it's not God who shuts man out—rather it's man who shuts himself out. I repeat, the "Good News" of Jesus Christ is that any sin can be forgiven—even the sin of shutting God out of one's life if it is sincerely confessed. No sin, I say is beyond God's forgiveness if a person honestly feels guilty for it, confesses it, desires not to do it again and strives by the grace of God, to eliminate the sin from his life as quickly as possible. No sin brought before God in this spirit will ever go "unforgiven."

In conclusion, I simply say this. With the "Good News," there's also a "warning." It's wonderful—it's simply great to know that we can take any sin to God whatsoever—and if we're truly repentant, He'll forgive that sin through the Cross of Jesus Christ. But, my friends, there has also a very stern warning in the morning's message—and that is that like the so-called "religious" people of Jesus' day, we too can very easily become "immune" to the leading of God's Holy Spirit in our life. I don't care how long you've been a Christian. And I don't care how "good" you think you are—and I don't care how many so-called "religious" things that you do in your life—you are still capable of losing your capacity to be truly "open" and "receptive" to God's will and grace in our life. And just like with the Scribes and Pharisees, it could very likely be at a time when you would least expect it, at that time in your life, when you think of yourself as being "pretty darn good and religious."

Jesus said, "He who exalts himself shall be humbled and he who humbles himself shall be exalted." A very fitting warning, I think. St. Paul said, "Do not think of yourself more highly than you ought to think." He also said of himself, "I am the greatest of all sinners." A very good frame of mind, I would say, to be in, at all times. St. Peter said, "Lord, depart from me for I am a sinful man." The Psalmist prayed, "O God, if you would ever count up my sins, how could I ever deservingly stand before you?" No chance here, I would think, of ever "blaspheming" the Holy Spirit—not with this attitude. The question is, what is YOUR attitude, and MINE? Is it possible that you, or ever I, could be actually committing the "unforgivable" sin of shutting God's Holy Spirit out of our life without ever knowing it? Is it possible? My friends, if it wasn't possible, surely Jesus wouldn't have warned us about it. The only thing that I can suggest is that each of us do a little soul-searching here this morning before we take Holy Communion. Just remember this...because of what Jesus did on that Cross, you can rest assured that God will forgive any and every sin that you honestly and sincerely confess before Him. It us up to us though—God wants to forgive every sin. He wants to cleanse us completely. He wants to make us completely 100% new, but He can't, if, in our pride and self-righteousness, we shut Him out. It's up to us—not Him—us, my friends, US.

Amen.

1979

Born Anew—Daily

The religious experience fad has been a part of the all religions on earth. In the early days of America, it was what has come to be called, "The Great Awakening." John Wesley and his "circuit riders" were the force behind this movement. And then, more recently, we've had the "Jesus People" movement in the 1960's, and now today in the 70s, we have the "born again" Christian movement. Charles Colson of Watergate fame has written a book and made a movie on his "born again" experience. Then, of course, there's Anita Bryant—there's the Pat Boone family and scores of other celebrities including the President's own sister.

Now, let me ask you a question. How many of you know what a "born again" Christian IS? You know, I'm not really surprised, for you see, many people in the more traditional churches like us Lutherans, the Presbyterians, the Episcopalians, the Methodists, and even the Roman Catholics, I say, people from these more formal churches don't usually talk about their "religious experiences" in this kind of language. And yet, as we can see from today's Gospel Lesson, as well as in a good many other places in the Bible, being "born anew" is a very necessary religious experience. If you'll notice—Jesus didn't say, "Now I think it might be a pretty good idea—sometime—for you to consider the possibility of perhaps, under right circumstances, when you feel like it—of being "born anew." No, what Jesus said was that a person must be born again if he or she wants to enter the "Kingdom of God." You must be "born again."

Now—the question is—What does it mean to be "born again"? What's it like? And how can you and I know if we've been "born again"? Well, let me take a couple of minutes and try to answer these questions—and, maybe, in the process, we'll see why we Lutherans find this to be a rather foreign experience. You see, the problem is that we Lutherans, along with others in the more main-line churches—we have often been guilty of over-emphasizing the intellectual side of our faith—while often neglecting the more emotional side. What I'm saying is that Lutherans have traditionally been, more or less, a "head" religion group of believers over against those who are of the "heart." In other words, in the past we Lutherans, along with others, have stressed the necessity of knowing and understanding what we believe as a Christian, while some of the other Christian groups have been guilty of over-emphasizing the emotional side—the feeling for God in the heart.

Well, of course, the truth is that there's a need for both—a balance between the two—and the fact is that any time the majority of Christian groups begin to intellectualize their faith—while possessing little feeling about it—it's at that time that some special group comes along—like the Jesus People or the Born

Again Christians, or the Charismatics—and they begin to make the mistake of the other side. In other words, they begin to over-emphasize the significance of the "heart-felt" experiences—often to the point that they "feel" a lot more than then "think." For example, you have certain Christians today who spend so much time telling you about their own personal religious experience that you hear almost nothing at all about the action of God in Christ. You know, I even heard of one church in which the members spent so much time in giving their personal testimonies that there wasn't enough time in the service for the pastor to preach on God's Word. You see what I mean about keeping a proper balance between the two—between what we believe in our heads and what we feel in our hearts?

But, let's get back to what it means to be "re-born" and I mean what it means in the Bible itself—for, you see, in the original Greek language the expression "born anew" literally means to be "born from above"—that is, to be "born of God." So, in effect, what Jesus was saying to Nicodemus was that there's one "birth" that comes from our human or earthly parents, but that there still another "birth" that comes from God—from "above." So, you see, to be "re-born" or "born anew" simply means that God so enters our life and human experience, that we confess Him to be our Heavenly Father to whom we belong—and that we begin to "commit" our life to Him. Sounds a lot like what I said to the children this morning, doesn't it? Now here's where all the differences come in—because, you see, some people say that God has one special way in which he causes this "re-birth" in people—very dramatic, very emotional—very much like the "re-birth" or "conversion" of St. Paul in the Bible. In fact, many of these people say that unless you can name the day and hour and minute when you were "re-born," then you really haven't been "re-born." Now, here, you see, is where the emotional part of faith begins to "get out-of-balance"—for it's one thing, I say, to acknowledge that God does indeed work His "rebirth" in some people in a very dramatic, emotional way—where they can actually point to the exact moment that it occurred—and I must confess that I'm one of those who can do that—but it's quite another thing to say that all people must have this very same kind of a "re-birth" experience or it isn't "legitimate." I think that Jesus Himself was trying to say this when He said to Nicodemus that "the Wind"—and, by the way, in Greek, the word for "wind" and God's "spirit" are the same—so when He said that the "Wind" blows where it wills" and that "you don't know whence it comes or whither it goes"—He was saying, in a sense, that the Spirit of God "works in different people in different ways."

You see, what I'm saying is that God may very well bring a "new birth" to some people in a very "dramatic" and "emotional" and "life-shaking-manner"—but that it doesn't have to happen this way to all people. As the Hymn says, "God works in mysterious ways His wonders to perform." Like the Wind, God sometimes "touches" people with His Spirit in soft-gentle strokes—wherein they hardly even "feel" it—while for others He "blows" His Spirit upon them in hard and forceful ways—to the point that it about "knocks them off their feet." As I said—that's the way it came to me—my "re-birth"—but I'm not about to limit the working of God's Holy Spirit by saying that everyone has to be "re-born" the way I was. The important thing is—do we both believe in our minds and feel in our hearts that through Christ we now belong to God and that He is the

"Lord & Master" of our life? Now, we may not be able to tell people exactly when we had this "re-birth" or what lead us to it—but, I say, that's not really the important part of it—to know the "when" or the "where" or the "how"—but simply to know that it is—that it exists within us.

In fact, to be completely accurate, we would have to say that the Bible doesn't just speak of one "re-birth" but of "numerous re-births"—and, as a result, as Lutherans we believe as Luther did in a "daily re-birth." In the Small Catechism, Luther says that "day after day a new self must arise." In other words, "re-birth" may indeed have a beginning, but rather being a single event, it's more like a process that goes on and on, wherein the old sinful self is continually dying and the new spirit in Christ, the "new self" is being continually re-born. One book I read compared this process to that of the continuous birth and death of the cells in our body—a process which of course must occur if the body is to grow.

The point is, my friends, that spiritual "rebirth"—while sometimes quite dramatic and other times very subtle—"spiritual rebirth" is something that should happen to a Christian each and every day of their life. As someone once said, "Just as we can't live on the air we breathed yesterday, so we can't live on yesterday's faith." Daily renewal. Daily rebirth. Daily allowing God to touch us with His Holy Spirit—that we might grow and become the kind of persons that we have the potential to become. The question is—in what way, in what life experiences is God trying to bring "rebirth" into your life—and then, the question, are you working for or against it? Just remember—some people have to be out on a limb before they'll turn-over a new leaf...which should only serve as a reminder to us that God does indeed "move in mysterious ways His wonders to perform." And finally, may those familiar words of Psalm 51 be on our lips each and every day of our lives—the words:

> *Create in me a clean heart, O God,*
> *and put a new spirit within me.*
> *Cast me not away from thy presence,*
> *and take not thy Holy Spirit from me.*
> *Restore to me the joy of thy salvation.*
> *and uphold me with a willing spirit.*

I say—pray that prayer daily and then allow God to do his "re-birthing" in your life—whether you're actually conscious of it always or not—and I promise you my friend you will indeed experience the Kingdom of God.

Amen.

January 31, 1988

God's Use of Church Buildings

I am honored that your pastor asked me to preach at this Service here this evening. On behalf of the Northwest Marion County Ministerial Association, which I am here representing, I congratulate you on your new church building. It is, truly, a beautiful place. You should be very proud of it. I think that I can speak for all of the pastors of our Ministerial Association when I say that we are very proud of Reverend Minor and his accomplishments here at Progressive Missionary Baptist Church. By the way, in my 28 years of ministry, I think that this is the very time that I have ever preached in a Baptist church, I think that Martin Luther would be proud of me. I know that Martin Luther King would be.

Now there are several questions, I think, which arise as a congregation enters into a new church building after a period of intense planning and construction. One of those questions is where do we go from here? What'll we do for an "encore"? And the other question is "What indeed is a church building for?"

I believe, my friends, that the answers to these two questions are about the same. Indeed, I believe that it all starts with that mission which our Lord Jesus Christ gave to His Holy Church when He said—as you heard this evening in that lesson from the 28th chapter of St. Matthew—"Go, therefore, and make disciples of all nations—baptizing them in the name of the Father, and of the Son, and of the Holy Spirit—teaching them all that I have commanded you."

As you all well-know, this is known as the "Great Commission." Indeed, my friends, this is where we go to get the answer to our questions: "Where does the congregation of Progressive Missionary Baptist Church go from here?"…"What do they do, now, with this new building they have?" Well, my friends, if Jesus himself was standing up here I believe He would say, "Remember My people what I told you long ago…Go out and make disciples. Take care of my sheep. Love one another as I have loved you. Be My witnesses to the ends of the earth. Do it unto the least of them as unto me." I believe that's what he would say.

Let me ask you yet another question…What do these two familiar hymns have in common in their titles? "Onward Christian Soldiers" and "Lead On O King Eternal"? What about forward motion? "Onward Christian Soldiers," "Lead On O King Eternal." My friends, in reading the Bible you will never find God "standing still"—"resting on His laurels" so to speak. God, I say, is forever in motion—and it's always forward-motion—never backward. Indeed, in Holy Scripture, our Lord God is forever telling His people to "go" or to "move-on." He said it to Abraham as He told Abraham to go from his home in Babylonia to the land of Canaan. He said it to the Israelites, as

He told His chosen people to go-back to Canaan, after their years of slavery in Egypt. And then, if you'll remember, he also said it much later to the Apostle Paul in a dream one night—after Paul had finished his mission in Ephesus—God called out to Paul and told him "to come over here to Macedonia." In other words, "Paul, you've completed for me what I wanted you to do over there, and, now, I've got another job over here for you to do." The point is of course, my friends, that no sooner has a Christian—or a Church—completed one task or mission for the Lord, then he calls that Christian or that Church to yet another task or mission. Indeed, ladies and gentlemen, there is simply "no resting on one's laurels" for the one who follows Jesus Christ.

By the way—you did know, did you not—that it was over 200 years before the first Christians ever had a real church building like you have and like most of us have? Indeed—because of the severe persecution of Christians during those first couple hundred years—our forefathers of faith had to meet and worship wherever they could—in private houses, in caves, in catacombs—wherever they could come together with the slightest attention or notice. And, of course, you also know—do you not—that the "Church" of Jesus Christ—is not really a place or a building, but rather the people themselves who believe in the Lord Jesus Christ. As the apostle Peter said in the other lesson for this evening—"You who believe in Christ, you are a chosen race, a royal priesthood, a holy nation. God's Own People—called to declare his wonderful deeds."

As someone once wrote, "The Church is never a place, but always a People. Never a Fold, but always a Flock. Never a sacred Building, but always a Believing Assembly."

Unfortunately, I'm afraid, there are some Christians who think more of the building in which they meet—than they do of the mission and of the ministry that the building is intended to fulfill. In other words, there are some Christians who, very sadly, look upon the church building as an "end in itself"—rather than simply as a "means to a greater end." Indeed, I've heard of people like this being labeled as having "an Ediface complex"…and I didn't say Oedipus. An "Ediface" complex. You see, that's when the Church building—the Edifice itself—comes to mean more to a Christian than the mission and the ministry—that are to be served by the building.

I remember a young lady in my very first church down in Bellevue, Kentucky who told me after we'd done some rather extensive remodeling and expansion of the church, that she just wouldn't be able to come to church anymore, because we'd changed the location of the entrance, and it just wouldn't seem like the church any longer. Still another member said that since we have removed the wall painting of Christ praying in the Garden of Gethsemane from behind the altar, that they just wouldn't be able to pray in the church any longer. Again, that is called "the Ediface complex." I certainly hope that none of you have that dreaded disease.

What then IS a church building really for? Well, ladies and gentlemen, I see the purpose of any church building being "two-fold." First, to aid and assist the individual Christian in his or her own personal spiritual walk with the Lord—and then, secondly, to aid, assist, and equip those same Christians in the mission that they have—to go and take the Gospel into all the world around them.

A man by the name of John Havlik wrote a little book once

about the church and in it he said that "The Pharisees in the time of Jesus said, 'Come to the temple'—while Jesus Himself said, 'Go-out into world.'"

For the Pharisees, Havlik wrote, "The center of religious activity was in the place of worship—in the temple or in the synagogue. While for Jesus," he said, "the center of all religious activity was in the streets."

He went on to write "That, indeed, if Jesus returned to earth—not for His Final visit, but just to see how things were going, He might just, come to some of church services. But," Havik says, "that if we wanted to find Him, we'd probably have to look for Him out in the streets where He'd be holding some 'dirty' children on His knee and talking to them about God's love."

And, finally, Havlik writes, "The Pharisees said, 'Come to Jerusalem. Come to the temple. Come to us.' While Jesus," Havlik writes, "said, 'Go into all the world. Go to those in need around you. Go and share My love.'"

Ladies and gentlemen, whether you be members of this congregation or of another, let me urge you to remember what has been said here this evening. And, finally, remember this…While there have always been those religious people who have moved heaven and earth to build and maintain their religious structures and institutions, let us always remember, my friends that Jesus died to reach people with His saving grace. In other words, for some believers it is the brick and mortar and the institutions that really matter, while for Jesus, my friends, it is the people that matter. The People.

Lord, may this building, indeed be used for the "People"— for the people here, for those out in the streets…and for those in all the world.

Amen.

April 12, 1998 (Easter Sunday)

Resurrection...A Present Reality

Resurrection. When you hear that word, what do you think of? Resurrection. I'm curious. I want all of you who might be thinking of something in the future when you hear that word—you know like what happens after we die—like the Resurrection of the Dead, the Final Judgment—things like that. If you're thinking future Resurrection, I want you to raise your hand.

And now all of you who were thinking about the very first Resurrection—when Jesus "arose from the dead"—on that first Easter Sunday—all of you raise your hand. Anyone left—besides those not thinking at all? Was anyone, when I said the word Resurrection, thinking about something in the present—in the here and now?

You know, I'm not really surprised...for I think it's only natural that when the word "Resurrection" is mentioned, people usually only think of something that WILL happen—like the

"Resurrection to come" OR of that very first "Resurrection" long ago when Jesus "arose from the dead." But I say almost never is the word "Resurrection" associated with something that happens right now. In other words, very seldom I'm afraid, do you and I think of "Resurrection" as a present reality. And my friends, that's precisely what I would like for us to think about for a few minutes here this morning. That is, those resurrections that God gives to us here and now.

By the way, the dictionary defines "resurrection" or "to resurrect" as "to bring back to life," "to revive," "to restore life after death has occurred." Now remember that definition. Obviously then, by definition, there can only be a Resurrection where there has been a death preceding it. In other words, very simply my friends, there can be no Resurrection without a death. No Death. No Resurrection. It's just as simple as that.

And what I would like to suggest to you, my friends, is that there are indeed a good many Resurrections that I believe God is bringing about—or attempting to bring about—in many of the lives that are here today. The bringing of the new life out of that which has died. The renewing of lives. The reviving of lives. The Resurrection to a brand-new life. Indeed, my friends, there is I believe in each of us something old, which in fact, needs to die in order that God might bring to us a Resurrection. That is a new life. Or, at least, a new part to our life. But again, just remember that, indeed, there can be no Resurrection without a death.

By the way, what is it in your life right now, that perhaps, needs reviving? Are there some dead areas in your life which indeed need to die, so that God can breathe some newness into them? Think about that for a moment.

Maybe there's something in a certain relationship that you're in right now—that is pretty dead. With a mate, with a friend, with a relative. You kids, with your parents. And maybe, that relationship needs a big Resurrection right now. Again, just remember that in order for new life to occur, something first has to die.

Or maybe some of you, right now are feeling the need for a newness in your person. In the core of your being. Something, maybe, that you don't really like about yourself. Something that you know really needs to die. If you are ever to be more mature, more secure, or just all-around better able to cope with things in life. Again, remember that something must first die for this newness to come.

Or maybe someone out there is seeking a Resurrection to their physical well-being. But they know that in order for this to occur, they must first allow a death to come to certain bad health-habits which they have now have. Could that be any of you? Or maybe, just maybe some of you have recently been through a kind of Resurrection without even realizing it. Thinking about it know, have you perhaps had some kind of a God-given Resurrection lately? Or are you may be going through one right now?

My friends, the great and wonderful truth of Easter is that our great and wonderful God has the power to take that which is dead, totally dead, and bring new life out of it. He did it with Christ Jesus. Indeed, He will do it with those who die, believing in Jesus. And my friends, He will also do it for you and for me—right here and now—if we will but call upon Him to give us that new life-power. Do you believe that? I know that I do. I've seen Him do it many times over in people's lives. In my life as well. Bringing new life out of that which was dead. Remember Resurrection is God's business.

A story comes to mind...a Lutheran college student had become despondent about her life. So despondent, in fact, that she had actually become suicidal. Her campus pastor had referred her to a psychiatrist, but she had refused to go. Late one night in her dormitory room, she sought to take her life. The residence hall advisor called the pastor who went immediately to the hospital where he found her virtually comatose. He sat there with her for what seemed like hours listening to her moans from the depths of her despair. Now he didn't know whether she could hear him or not, but he took her hand in his and said to her over and over again—My dear, God loves you...God loves you...God loves you. Suddenly she opened her eyes and asked in a rather groggy voice, "Oh Pastor, is that really true? Can God love somebody like me?" The pastor squeezed her hand and said, "You know God sent Christ Jesus to die for you. God loves you that much." From that moment on, this young student began to recover from her near fatal experience. Indeed, from that very experience itself, there in the hospital with her pastor, this young lady began to experience not only a renewal of interest in life, but also in her own self-worth as a child of God. You see, my friends, God had LOVED this young lady back to life. And that, I say, was a Resurrection in the here and now.

You know what? I bet that God has a place in your life right now that He's trying to revive or bring new life. You know, He's got the power to do it—if you'll just let him. Will you?

Amen.

December 1998

Let Us Return to Bethlehem

As we gather together on this night before Christmas, I'm sure that many different thoughts fill the minds of those assembled here. Some of you I'm sure are thinking about how hectic it has been in the past few weeks getting ready for the "big day" tomorrow. Others of you are thinking about the things that you've still got to do when you get home after tonight's service is over. And I'm sure that a good many of you are thinking about tomorrow itself—what you're going to get in your Christmas presents. Or maybe the meal that you've got to fix. Or the trip that you're going to take for the day to the home of your loved ones and friends. A few of you I hope are thinking about the real meaning of Christmas—the birth of the Savior—the coming into the world of the Lord God himself. The incarnation. God sharing our human flesh with us—that he might redeem us and save us.

And yet how difficult is it not to become preoccupied with all of these externals of Christmas, right? Indeed, how terribly easy it is with all of the commercialization of Christmas to forget the babe wrapped in swaddling clothes. To forget all together that Christmas is in fact the birthday of the Christ child. Of course, we know it—but we forget it, don't we? The world crowds it out. We understand the story—but we sadly somehow lose the true feeling for it. It gets all lost in the rush, am I not correct?

But tonight, in these next few moments we are going to return to Bethlehem—and there we are going to try to re-capture the true feeling that we all know that we should indeed feel on this most holy of nights. Let us return then, to Bethlehem—and as we do, we see three lonely figures moving ever so slowly along the path which leads to Bethlehem. One a man, one a woman and the other that of a donkey bearing the form of the woman. They appear to be very tired. As if they have come a long way. And now, we see that they have come to the edge of the town of Bethlehem. Yes, we can see them more clearly now. It's Joseph and Mary. They've come all the way from Nazareth—and Mary is just about ready to have her baby—the baby promised to her by God himself. The baby which they have been instructed to call "Jesus."

Oh, by the way—doesn't the sanctuary look awesome tonight with all these special Christmas decorations. The trees. All the poinsettias. It's really a great setting for a candlelight service, isn't it? Oh, excuse me, I forgot the story that I was telling you. Let's go back to Bethlehem.

The some 80 miles that Joseph and Mary had traveled had taken their toll on the expectant mother. But since it was late at night—and many of the other people who had come to Bethlehem for the same reason as Joseph—that is—to enroll themselves on the census decreed by Caesar Augustus—since so many of them were already settled in the town—Joseph and Mary discovered that they could not find a place in which to stay in the town's inn. It was all filled-up.

I bet that some of you have a filled-up house this week-end, too, don't you? Indeed, I can see that we have some visitors here this evening. You know, it's always nice at this time of year, isn't it, to get together with our family and friends? Oh, of course, it's a lot of extra work and sometimes the weather isn't too good for traveling, but what's Christmas without lots of people around? Especially—dear friends and loved ones. Oh sorry—there I go again—forgetting my story. Well, back to Bethlehem...

Now, since there was no room in the inn for Joseph and Mary, the keeper of the inn—seeing the condition of Mary suggested to them that they take one of the stalls in his stable where they might keep warm and be at least half-way comfortable. Now, the Bible story really doesn't say anything about the innkeeper offering them any food but then I suppose that they probably had a little bit left from their trip. But I really don't think that Mary cared too much about eating—the way that she probably felt.

Oh, speaking of food—that's another thing I really like about Christmas...you know all the good food that people cook. And those Christmas cookies and candy. I think that some of you already know just how much I personally like cookies. In fact, when Liz and I got married, we had cookies at our wedding reception instead of cake. I don't know about you, but I always seem to gain a few pounds over the holidays. Oops, there I go again—getting away from my story of Jesus and his birth. Well, back again to Bethlehem we go...

It was in a lowly stable surrounded by farm animals that God first made his appearance to us in human form. Mary placed her son in a manger—that is, in the trough from which the animals ate. And she wrapped him up in a swaddling cloth—which was simply a large square of cloth with a bandage-like strip coming off from one corner. First, she laid the baby Jesus in the square cloth—and then she took the long strip and wound it around and around him. Remember, no fancy hospital. No clean bed. No germ-free gown—just a lowly stable. This my friends is how God first came to earth. In a common courtyard to common parents.

It's very late at night, now—and as Joseph and Mary sit there with their new Son—God's promised Messiah. We see a small group of people beginning to approach the stable in which the baby Jesus lies. It's a band of Shepherds—a few small boys, and a hand-full of men. Oh, yes, they heard about the birth of Jesus—for the Angels of God appeared unto them in the field and told them, "Fear not: for, behold we bring you good tidings of great joy. For unto you is born this day in the City of David, a Savior, who is Christ the Lord." Yes, these shepherds have come to pay their respects to the new "king" of the Jews—God's appointed "Messiah"—his Savior—for whom God's chosen people have awaited thousands of years. And with this tribute from the shepherds—we are told that sometime later three wise men came from the east—bearing their personal gifts for the Christ child.

And of course, while we are talking about gifts, I hope that all of you will also be pleased with the gifts that you'll be receiving tomorrow as well. And I bet that all you boys and girls can hardly wait until tomorrow when you get up—and open all those presents under your Christmas tree. Right kids? Boy, it sure takes a lot of money to get through Christmas, doesn't it? And yet it's really all worth it—to see the kids happy, isn't it? Christmas is maybe the happiest time of the year—don't you think? Parties, friends, loved ones, lots of good things to eat—and all those presents. It's great, isn't it? But, there I go again—forgetting my story. Oh well, it's getting late anyhow—(look at my watch)—and besides, we can return to Bethlehem again next year. Now what was it that I was saying about having a good time at Christmas? The PARTIES, the PRESENTS and the FOOD and EVERYTHING?!!

Let us now sing the hymn #279, "O Little Town of Bethlehem."

March 2004 (Lent)

The Good News in a Single Sentence

The Bible text for my sermon this morning is taken from our second lesson for today from the apostle Paul's Second letter to the Church at Corinth, II Corinthians 5:21...and this is from the living Bible translation. And it reads once again, "For God took the sinless Christ and poured into him our sins." Then in exchange, Paul writes, "God poured his own goodness into us." That my dear friends, I would suggest to you is the Good News of Jesus Christ in a single sentence.

Let me repeat it one more time..."For God took the sinless Christ and poured into him our sins." In fact, my friends, that is what the Lenten season is all about. Indeed, this is a message that I believe you and I need to hear again and again.

A Dr. Kenneth Foreman writes about our text from II Corinthians, "Here is a truth," he says, "that is almost too strange to be true." To think that God in Christ would come so far over to our side—that he not only became human—but he actually took the place of the human sinner. Christ himself Foreman says, "was without sin, but for us he was made to be sin." And then Dr. Foreman says—and I like this—"As He (referring to Christ) took our place, he then gave us his place."

Do you know what I think of when I hear something like this? I think of what they call a movie stuntman. You know that person who is a "stand-in" or "substitute" for the real actor. You know a stuntman is the person takes all of the falls and punches. The one who performs the really dangerous acts on behalf of the more famous actor, so that they themselves won't get hurt.

The point is you see, that Jesus was, in fact, our "stand-in." In other words, Jesus took our place in Hell. That's why we say that "he descended into Hell" in the creeds. And by so doing, He who was WITHOUT sin (Christ Jesus) took the punishment and the suffering for all of us upon Himself.

Indeed, my friends, the prophet Isaiah "foretold" of this hundreds of years before it actually happened. As it said in our first lesson Isaiah Chapter 53, "He was despised and rejected by men, yet he was pierced for our transgressions. He was crushed for our iniquities. The punishment that brought us peace, was upon Him. And by his wounds, we are healed. The Lord has laid on Him the iniquity of us all."

There again you see is the whole story of our eternal salvation. Christ is the holy sinless one. And we are the sinful, guilty ones. Indeed, we are the ones who in fact deserve to be punished. And yet, on the Cross of Calvary, Christ becomes our "Savior," in that He comes and takes our place on the Cross and He then gives us his.

I read somewhere, where it said that Christ took MY HELL that I might have HIS HEAVEN. I like that. That about says it all doesn't it. Now that, my friends, is the Gospel in the just 10 words—Christ took MY HELL that I might have HIS HEAVEN.

Back about 40-45 years ago, when I was serving a church over in a little town called Elwood, Indiana—when I was asked by the Elementary School Principal there to present a short "Good Friday" message for all of the children in the School—that was when Pastors could do that kinda thing in the schools. Well, I really wanted to convey to the children the meaning of Christ's death on the Cross. And I wanted to do so with words that they would understand. And so, I told them this story...

There was a class of 5th graders, who one day, had their teacher tell them that she was going to leave the room for a few minutes and that they were to do their work and be quiet until she returned. Well, while she was gone out of the room, several of the children got into an eraser throwing contest. And in the process, the teacher's prized crystal flower vase sitting on her desk, just happened to get in the way of one of the flying erasers. The vase fell to the floor in pieces. And just as the crash could be heard throughout the room, the teacher returned.

Well, obviously, she wanted to know who had been responsible for this mischievous act that had resulted in the breakage of her prized vase. But no one would speak up. And so, she warned the class that unless the guilty child came forward and confessed, the whole class would have to stay after school for 60 minutes—one full hour. Well, it just so happened that the very boy who had thrown the eraser was the same young lad who was scheduled to run in the school's track meet right after school was out. And to make matters worse, this particular boy was the fastest runner that the school had. And besides, the track meet only lasted for one hour. And when several of the children mentioned the track meet to the teacher (since a number of the other children were also involved in the meet), the teacher simply said, "That's just too bad. For unless the guilty one confesses, the whole class stays."

Well, it also so happened that the best friend of this one boy who was the guilty one knew what it meant to his friend and to the rest of the class—indeed, to the whole school, to have him be able to run in the meet. And so, even though this friend had not even been one of the mischievous children—indeed was completely innocent—he nevertheless chose to stand-up confessing that he himself had done it.

Well I then told the children in the assembly room, that this innocent child then took the punishment in place of his friend. And that this in fact, was what Jesus did for us, when he died on the Cross. That Jesus, the innocent one took the place, took the suffering, took the punishment that we the guilty ones really deserve.

I think, I hope, that the children understood what I was trying to say to them that day. And I hope that you do too. It is an old, old, story, I know my friends. You've heard it before. And hopefully, you'll hear it many more times before you die.

In closing then, I would like to ask you to do something for me. I would like for all us to take just a moment of silence to gaze at that cross over there. And as you do so, ask yourself in a quiet introspective way—"Lord, what does it mean to me that you died for me?" Ask yourself that question, "Lord, what does it mean to me that you died for me?" I say, really think about that for a moment. Let whatever thoughts come into your mind, COME. "Lord, what does it mean to me that you died for me?"

Amen.

November 4, 2007

Where Do We Go from Here?

(A pep talk to the congregation after the Senior Pastor had left)

I remember a seventeen-year-old a number of years back who had been named the Captain of his football team for one game. A game in which they were huge underdogs having lost the first three games of their season. The other team was undefeated. This young seventeen-year-old got his team together before they left on the bus to play the other team on their home field. And before they left, he got them all together and gave them a good old-fashioned pep talk, telling them that they, indeed, were better than an 0-3 team. He told them that night, that they were going to show everyone just how good a football team they really were. Well, that team, my friends, was so fired-up that at half-time they led 20-0! Oh, by the way that seventeen-year-old was yours truly. And this morning I'm going to give yet another one of my good old-fashioned pep-talks! The sermon title for this morning is simply, "Where do we go from here?"

The answer is wherever God directs us to go! Before that first Palm Sunday long ago, as it reads in Matthew 21:6, "the disciples went and did as Jesus had directed them." The disciples did as Jesus directed them! In Proverbs 16:9 it says, "The human mind plans the way, but the Lord directs the steps." Where do we go from here? It is pretty obvious isn't it? We're going to go where the Lord directs us.

And how are we going to know where God is directing us? Well, let me hear your answer to that question. How are we going to know? Say it out loud! I think I hear a lot of "prayer" answers. Yes, we are all going to have to do a lot of praying in the weeks and months ahead aren't we? Lord, show us the way to go! Lord, direct us to the Pastor whom You want to lead us in the years ahead. Lord, help us to achieve the goals that we have set for ourselves with respect to our building and ministry expansion. And, Lord, raise-up for us in our midst at this time the leaders and the servants that we will need to do all of this. Lord, show us the way to go!

You know, maybe in addition to asking, "Where do we go from here?" maybe we should also ask, "With whom do we go?" Again, the answer I think should be quite obvious. But you know sometimes, my friends, even the faithful forget. I am reminded of the time when Moses was directed by God to lead the Israelites into the Promised Land, out of the wilderness, in which they had been traveling for some forty years. Now, you see, Moses knew that the Promised Land was cram full of peoples who would oppose the Israelites coming into their land to settle there. In other words, the Israelites were going to be the trespassers and Moses knew this. Believe me, this was not a direction from God that Moses was looking forward to. Indeed, that's when Moses said to God in Exodus 33:12, "Lord, You have told me to lead these people into the land You promised them, but You have not let me know whom You will send with me." And you know what God's answer was? "My presence will go with you." I repeat God said, "My presence will go with you." With whom do we, as a congregation, go in the months and years ahead? Well, my friends, it is that very same God who went with Moses. In other words, my friends, wherever God directs us and leads us He will be right there with us every step along the way. Of course, you knew that didn't you? But I think, my friends, that we are going to have to remind each other of that quite often in the days ahead! That whatever we are doing, we are not doing it alone!

And now to some very practical matters. First off, I want you to know that as your Interim Pastor I will not be a full-time pastor like Pastor Diehl. In other words, I will not be putting-in the same hours that he did. No interim pastor can ever do what a full-time "Called Pastor" does. And, not only will I be unable to do all of the things that Pastor Diehl did, and please hear this, I will not necessarily do things the same way that Pastor Diehl did them. There will be a few changes. In fact, interim pastors are actually supposed to help a congregation get used to the new ways of a new pastor whom they will be getting in the not too distant future.

Now, having said that, I need to also tell you that I'm going to be relying on you to do a lot of the ministry that God has called us to do here at Shepherd of the Valley. But I also want you to know that in my most humble opinion we have some very strong Lay leadership here in this congregation. Indeed, it is as strong as I've experienced in my almost fifty years of pastoral ministry. I believe that this is one of our congregation's strengths! The leadership of you and you and you!

I also believe that in order for this congregation to fulfill the mission and the ministry that God has given to us we need to expand our facilities. And we need to move ahead as quickly as possible. Only God of course knows the precise time-table for this but we need to be open to His guidance and direction. Indeed, at our congregational meeting on December 9th we will be challenged to continue to heed God's call in this direction.

Now this I promise to you. I will continue to be your "Support Pastor" until God calls a new strong full-time Pastor to lead you into this expanded ministry that I believe He has called you to fulfill in the years ahead.

In conclusion you know that football game that I mentioned at the beginning of this sermon? Well, we lost the game, 21-20! And you know why we lost it? Simply because we lost our momentum! Well, my friends, if I have anything to say about it, we will not lose our momentum here at Shepherd of the Valley simply because we do not have a full-time Lead Pastor! Besides, this is not a game. This is the "kingdom of God" that we are talking about here. And by the grace of God and with His inspiration and empowerment we are going to move-ahead and we are going to succeed in fulfilling God's will for this congregation! Aren't we? And all of God's people said loudly....

AMEN!

September 16, 2012

Oh, What a Relief It Is!

Have you ever thought what indeed it would feel like to stand before God with all of your sins and failures laid bare without knowing anything at all about the Cross and about the forgiveness it offers? Can you imagine the feeling you would have? Indeed, my friends, if you and I can at times feel very guilty before God knowing about the Cross, just think how heavy the guilt would feel if we didn't know about it? In other words, can you imagine the dreadful feeling of fear that a person would have standing before God almighty with all of their life's sins revealed if they didn't know anything at all about the Cross?

Well, I think the writer of Psalm 130, which we read together today, captured something of this feeling when he wrote long ago, "If, O Lord, you should mark iniquities, Lord, who could stand?" In other words, he was saying "Lord, if you should add up all of our sins and offenses against You O Lord, who could ever stand there before you?" You know, I must say that I've actually thought about this, standing there before God right after I die or even right now, standing there with a book in each hand one recording all of the so-called good deeds in my life and the other listing all of my sins and failures. You better believe I'd be standing like this. (The heavy weight of the book of sins would cause me to tilt to one side.) Wouldn't you look this way as well?

But you know something? Even the Psalmist of old, although knowing nothing about the Cross of Jesus, the Psalmist still knew something about the grace of God. For right after he says, "Lord, who could stand," he then goes on to say, "But, Lord there is forgiveness with thee." Indeed, my friends, even though the Psalmist doesn't tell us in detail precisely how this forgiveness will come to us yet in his heart, he believes beyond a doubt that with God there is indeed forgiveness for all of his many sins.

I say again, the Psalmist didn't know precisely how God was going to make His forgiveness known and available to humankind, but you and I know how He did it, don't we? It was there on the cross wasn't it that God paid the price for all that forgiveness. Indeed, as it says in hymn 395 in our hymnal "Glory be to Jesus who in bitter pains poured for me the life-blood from His sacred veins." That was the price wasn't it? That God paid for the forgiveness for all of these, for my sins, for yours…indeed for the sins of the whole world! A pretty high price to pay, wasn't it?

Let me direct you now if I may to that scripture passage from Colossians (Colossians 2:13-14) that I read to you this morning. In that passage it said, "God has forgiven us all our sins by canceling the certificate of debt which was against us by nailing it to the cross of Christ." Now it is important to note here that the people who were reading this letter from the Apostle Paul knew exactly what Paul was talking about when he made reference to this "certificate of debt." For you see back in those days they actually had what they called certificates of debt. The Greek word was cheirographon. And what this was, was a handwritten I-O-U. It was a written-out debt that one person owed to another. Well it just so happens that the very word that was used for this kind of a debt, a cheirographon was the very same word that Paul used here in this letter to the Colossians.

What is really interesting is that when such a debt, this I-O-U, was paid off (cancelled out) back in those ancient days they would do so by taking this certificate of debt and marking upon it he Greek letter "CHI" which looks like this: X. The "X" you see was crossing out the debt. Well my friends, the Greek letter for CHI, this X just happens also to be the very first letter for the name of Christ in Greek. You have probably heard of the Greek letter CHI-RHO: ☧ You will often see these two letters transposed on top of each other on various chancel paraments. CHI- RHO… CHRIST-JESUS.

See the connection? Both the X and Christ symbol P with X on top of it…both of them crossing out, canceling the debt that is owed. Do you think maybe those Colossian Christians understood what Paul meant when he said that God canceled their debt of sin by nailing it to the cross of Christ? Maybe better than some of us do? Oh, what a relief it is to not only know about this great forgiveness that God offers to each of us. But to feel it deep down in here, in our heart!

A husband said to his wife one day, "Honey, why do you keep talking about my past mistakes and failures? I thought that you had forgiven and forgotten them." And his wife replied, "Oh, I have forgiven and forgotten but I just want to make sure that you don't forget that I've forgiven and forgotten!" Thank goodness God doesn't forgive like that!

Indeed, my dear friends let us thank God that when He forgives, He forgives as God is pictured forgiving in this following story. As it is told, there was this Pastor, a much loved man of God, yet a man who unfortunately carried the burden of a secret sin, a sin that he had committed many years before. Now this Pastor had indeed repented of this sin quite often, but like I mentioned earlier, he just couldn't yet feel forgiven deep down inside. Again, he knew it up here in his head, but he just couldn't feel it down here in his heart. Well it seems that in this Pastor's parish there was this woman who was a very deeply spiritual person and who claimed to have these visions wherein she actually spoke with Jesus person-to-person! Well as you can imagine the Pastor was quite skeptical about all of this. And so, to test the woman he said to her one day, "My dear lady the next time that you speak to Jesus I want you to ask Him what terrible sin it was that I committed a long time ago." And the woman agreed to do so.

Well a few days later the Pastor asked the woman, "Well, did Jesus visit you in your dreams again?" "Yes, He did," she replied. "And did you ask Him about that terrible sin that I once committed?" he asked. And she replied softly "Yes, I did, Pastor." "Well, what did He say?" the Pastor asked. And the woman replied, "Well, He said, I don't remember."

Indeed, my friends the truth is what God forgives He also forgets. Oh, I say what a great relief it is to know, indeed to feel deep inside that in having canceled all of our sins, in having nailed them to the Cross, God not only forgives us our sins but that He also forgets all about them! Wiped clean from the slate of our life. Removed from His sight forever! Just think how it would feel if you were standing before God feeling quite unworthy and very guilty for all of your life's sins. And reading your mind and heart God said to you, "Fear not, my child. I don't even remember what your sins were."

My friends, what a relief it is to not only know that you are forgiven, but to really and truly feel forgiven deep down inside. Do you, friend, have that feeling? Or maybe you're one of those who indeed has a sin or two for which there is perhaps a lingering feeling of guilt? Well, my friend if you are one who needs that feeling of deep-down forgiveness, then try this. As you come forward in a few minutes to receive Holy Communion bring that sin which still plagues you from time to time with you. Look up at the cross as you stand up here and then in your mind just nail that sin right to the cross. And then leave it there, leave it there for good. Oh, what a relief it will be!

Amen.

2013

Already Forgiven— Even Before Asking

Did you know that even before you were born all of the sins that you were to ever commit in your life those sins were already forgiven before you were born? Did you know that? Which of course also means, you see that God has already forgiven you as well of those sins which you will be committing tomorrow, the next day, even next year. In fact, He has already forgiven you of any and all sins that you will commit the rest of your life. Did you know that?

And did you know that God indeed actually forgives you and me even before we ask Him to forgive us? Did you know that God forgives us even if we don't ask Him to? The point is, you see that our asking to be forgiven does not in itself cause God to forgive us. In other words, we don't have to persuade or convince God to forgive us. Our repentance, our begging to be forgiven is not what causes God to forgive us. Because you see He has already forgiven us even before we ask.

Let me try to illustrate what I'm saying here. A little boy went out to play in his back yard one day. But before he left the house, his mother warned him to be very careful of her potted plants that she had placed near the fence to get some sun. The little boy said that he would, as he rushed out into the yard to play. Well as it so happened the little boy was playing with his dog and he was throwing a stick for the dog to retrieve and to return to him. But on this one occasion the stick accidentally went right into the middle of his mother's potted plants. And of course, the dog went right in after it, knocking over and breaking several of his other's prized plants in the process.

Well immediately the little boy ran into the house and told his mother what had happened, only he failed to tell her that it was his stick throwing which had caused the dog to knock over and break her plants. In other words, he made it sound as if the dog had done it all on his own. You see he just knew that his mother would be terribly upset with him especially after warning him the way she did.

But before the day was out, the lie began to get to the little boy. And so, as he was getting ready for bed, he decided to tell her the truth. And he did. The whole story. The complete truth. And afterwards added, "Mom will you please forgive me?" To which his mother replied "Honey, I already have. You see," she said, "I was watching out the window while you were playing with the dog and I saw you accidently throw the stick into the flowers. And even though I was hurt and disappointed in you for what had happened, I forgave you right then. But honey," she said, "I'm very pleased and proud of you that you asked me to forgive you, because now," she said, "you can feel forgiven even though you would have actually had my forgiveness had you not asked for it."

I say to you my friends if an understanding, loving, human mother can forgive in this manner how much more can a heavenly father forgive! I don't know about you, my friends, but it is very comforting to me to occasionally stop and remind myself that indeed my Heavenly Father has already forgiven me of all the sins that I have committed against Him even before I ask Him to do so! Indeed, even if I don't ask Him, He has still already forgiven them.

You see my friends we know this to be true simply because of what the Bible tells us about the Cross. Indeed, we are told in the Bible that the Cross "made payment" for all of the sins which had ever been or would ever be committed. In other words, when Jesus died on that Cross almost 2000 years ago in that one event right then and there, God forgave all human sins. Those which had been committed previously by all the people before Jesus lived. Those which were being committed at the time Jesus was alive, as well as, all of those sins which indeed would be committed after the Cross. You see, my friends this, the Cross is what causes God to forgive you and me. Not that we deserve His forgiveness. Not that we have enough goodness in us to barter with Him for His forgiveness. Not even that we ask Him for it. No, my friends, what causes God to forgive us is the life-giving sacrifice of Christ Jesus upon the Cross.

You see some people, very wrongly, have the idea that the Crucifixion simply made God into a more loving and forgiving God than He was before. Some people have the notion that the Cross simply made God's forgiveness more available to us but that we then still have to convince God somehow that He should forgive us. But you see, my friends this misses the whole point of the Cross. The Cross didn't simply make it easier to approach God to be forgiven. No, the Cross as it was happening was God's act of forgiving right then and there each and every sin of humankind which either had been or would be committed. And that is why we can say that God has already forgiven us even before we ask, even if we don't ask. When I am asked, "Pastor will God ever forgive me for what I have done?" my answer is "He already has my friend. He already has." My, what good news this is!

Now having said all of this, someone out there is thinking "Well, Pastor, why then does the Bible instruct us to ask for God's forgiveness if He has already given it to us?" Well, do you remember what the mother said to her little boy after he had confessed his sin and after she told him that she had already forgiven him? Do you remember her words? Remember her saying, "Honey I'm so pleased and so proud of you that you came to me and asked me to forgive you because," she said, "now that you have asked for my forgiveness you can now feel forgiven in your heart." In other words, my friends, our asking for God's forgiveness isn't for God's sake so that our asking will in effect give God a reason to forgive us. No, the asking of God for His forgiveness is for our sake so that we can feel forgiven and then go out and love and forgive others as God has loved and forgiven us.

You see just like the mother in our story God knows that you and I can become terribly weighed down by the guilt we feel for certain sins in our life. God knows that even though He has already forgiven us in Christ, He knows, I say, that you and I still need to feel forgiven in our hearts. And of course, you see it is in the asking to be forgiven that you and I appropriate and receive into ourselves that forgiveness which God has already bestowed upon us.

The important thing to remember there is that our asking for God's forgiveness in our prayer of confession does not in itself cause or make God forgive us. Just as our asking God to be with us does not make Him present. God is present; He is with us always whether we seek His Presence or not. And so, in the same way we actually have God's forgiveness whether we ask for it or not. On the other hand, to appropriate that forgiveness to receive it into our hearts and to be truly healed and renewed by it we must indeed ask for it in Jesus' Name.

"O God, please forgive me!" "My child I already have! But I am glad you asked, for now, you can feel forgiven and you can go forth and forgive others as I have forgiven you!"

Amen.

April 6, 2014

And They Placed a Crown of Thorns on His Head

Anyone remember the old expression…"Boy, is that a thorn in my side?" Well, believe it or not my friends, that expression actually comes from a passage in the Bible, from the Book of Numbers in the Old Testament. Number 33:55 to be exact…wherein it speaks there of one's enemies as being a thorn in their side. You see, back in biblical days the word thorn or thorns was used as a symbol for something that was highly undesirable in a person's life. In fact, this goes all the way back to the Garden of Eden story wherein thorns and thistles are identified as "the most undesirable yield of the soil." By the way have you ever put your hand into a thorn bush or a thistle tree? Quite an undesirable experience, huh?

And why, you may ask, why all of this talk about thorns and thistles? Well, as you can probably guess from the sermon title, my message for this morning is in fact going to focus on that crown of thorns which was placed on our Lords head on that day of His crucifixion. In fact, I read about that occasion in my Gospel Lesson for today which is the only place in the Bible that tells us of this crown of thorns placed on Jesus' head. Matthew 27:29…The only place where the crown of thorns is mentioned…With a reed placed in His hand, they jeered and mocked Him saying, "Hail King of the Jews!" After which they spat on Him, stripped Him of His robe and led Him away to crucify Him.

My friends, what I would like for us to see here this morning are three very important reminders about suffering and about Christ's suffering and about ours. First then, let us be reminded of the great price that God in Christ paid for the forgiveness of our sins and for the free gift of eternal life in His heavenly kingdom. In other words, my friends, in the spiritual realm of things the Bible tells us, there was indeed a cost that is a price to be paid for the sins of humankind. Or, to put it yet another way, if you and I are to not suffer a punishment after we die for all of our many sins, the Bible tells us that someone else then must indeed suffer in our place. It says in Isaiah 53:5, "He was wounded for our transgressions. He was bruised for our iniquities. Upon him was the chastisement that made us whole and with his stripes we are healed."

Back in the early 1900's (over 100 years ago) a woman had been traveling in Europe and she came across a very valuable tapestry and since she and her husband were quite wealthy she wired him back in the states on the telegraph and asked him if she could purchase it even though it cost about $25,000 dollars (about $100,000 dollars in today's money). Well his reply back over the telegraph in four simple words was "No! Price too high!" But then when she returned from her trip with the tapestry her husband wanted to know why she had disregarded his reply and she showed him the telegraph cable which read "No price too high."

My dear friends for your eternal salvation and for mine, God thought that no price was too high! Even the price of the suffering and death of His only begotten Son! I say then let us be reminded here this morning as we contemplate that crown of thorns placed on Christ's head...let us be reminded, I say of that great price paid for each of us by our Lord and Savior Jesus Christ. Indeed, there was no price too high for God to give to you and to me His great and merciful love, to forgive us and to restore us to Himself for eternity. I say again "No price was too high."

And now let us shift our focus for a moment to our own suffering. And obviously as we do so, we can quickly see that in comparison to Christ's suffering on the cross, our suffering is very small. And yet how often do we hear, even from Christian people, such statements as "Doesn't God know that I can't take any more of this?" "Why doesn't He rid me of all of my pain and suffering," or Why do I have so much pain in my life when people who are not even believers or as faithful to God as I am, have so little pain or suffering?" I say, haven't we all either said or heard statements like these?

A young man of 36 lay in his hospital bed dying of cancer. The doctors had not yet told him of his terminal illness and his wife wanted it that way. But one day, when the man was alone with his Pastor, he pressed the Pastor so hard for the truth that the Pastor decided to tell the man what he wanted to know. The Pastor, you see, felt that the man deserved to be able to put his house in order before that last day.

Well, at first the man's wife was very upset over this. Upset that her husband now knew about his approaching death. You see, she was afraid that it would disturb him too much to know about it and as she said to her husband one day, "Bill it is just that I hate to see you suffer so much." Well, Bill's reply to his wife was, "Mary, first I just know that God will indeed take very good care of you and the children after I die. And as for my suffering, even if I do have to suffer a lot before I die, I just know honey," he said, "that I will never have to suffer as much as my savior suffered for me on the Cross!"

The point is that regardless of how much pain and suffering you and I have to endure in this life, even if it is greater than many other people have to endure, it will still in no way compare with the pain and suffering endured for us by our Savior on His cross.

And, finally then, let us be reminded as the Holy Scriptures testify of how God indeed is able to take our human suffering, just as He did, with that of Christ's and in fact, work something good out of it. As someone said once, "If God could use such a horrible injustice as was done to Jesus by crucifying Him as a criminal, such a good and holy man to win humankind their eternal salvation then, surely, God can take and use any pain or suffering in my life and yours and work something good out of it." Or as someone else once said, "Hurt can, indeed, help us when God gets His hands on it." Do you believe that? If you don't maybe you need to look at the Cross a little longer.

A crown of thorns! Yes, my friends Jesus had His! And in many different ways, you and I will have to wear a crown of thorns in our lives as well. But I say let us just remember three things about those crowns of thorns. Let us remember first that had it not been for Christ's crown of thorns, for His great suffering, you and I would never ever be able to see heaven! Secondly, let us remember that no pain or suffering that we will ever have will in any way ever compare with the pain and suffering that Christ endured for us. And finally and thirdly, let us remember that if God can indeed work something good out of the murder of the world's only sinless man then, surely, my friends, He can work something good out of anything bad that happens to you and to me. Right? And they placed a crown of thorns on His head. Sure, it hurt but just look at what God can do with hurt!

Amen.

December 28, 2014

It Is No Longer I Who Live But Christ Who Lives Within Me

It was late one Saturday evening in 1957, April 20th, I think. I was in prayer lying in bed tossing and turning and I finally said, "OK, God I'll become a pastor." It has never been the same since. Now nearly 60 years later I'm saying, "Yes, God it is time, isn't it? I tried to retire almost 15 years ago but You wouldn't let me, but now You're saying, "It is time, it's time."

As many of you know since January 1, 2001, I have been officially retired from active service in the ordained ministry as the plaque hanging on my wall from the national church reads. But what do they know? For the past 14 years, in my retirement, I have served actively in at least six congregations.

It was exactly this time of year between Christmas and New Year's, when Jeff, Kathy, and family were visiting us, as they are now, when I received a call from Bob Jansic. Bob, do you remember that phone call? Bob wanted to know if I would be interested in coming back to Trinity as their interim pastor. I was, at that time, winding up my interim ministry in Massillon and to once again make a long story short, everything just fell into place and here we are almost four years later. When I say that everything just fell into place, it was precisely that which convinced Liz and me that indeed God wanted us to be here.

I have never doubted for a moment that this is where God wanted me to be as I close out my pastoral ministry for good this time. I would now like to take a few minutes to explain to you the significance of the Bible passages that have been placed in your bulletin this morning and read to you by Kathy and Tami. Please take them out now so that you have them in front of you as I tell why they are there.

Galatians 2:20
...and it is no longer I who live, but it is Christ who lives in me. And the life I now live in the flesh I live by faith in the Son of God, who loved me and gave himself for me.

I chose the passage from Galatians 2:20 to be at the top my list and to have part of it on the screen simply because it is this passage that I chose right after my decision in April 1957 to become an ordained pastor. I felt at that time that this particular verse from the pen and heart of the Apostle Paul reflected exactly the way I also felt. I felt it was no longer I who was living, but Christ who now lived within me.

Psalm 27

The Lord is my light and my salvation; whom shall I fear? The Lord is the stronghold of my life; of whom shall I be afraid?

When evildoers assail me to devour my flesh—my adversaries and foes—they shall stumble and fall.

Though an army encamp against me, my heart shall not fear; though war rise up against me, yet I will be confident.

One thing I asked of the Lord, that will I seek after: to live in the house of the Lord all the days of my life, to behold the beauty of the Lord, and to inquire in his temple.

For he will hide me in his shelter in the day of trouble; he will conceal me under the cover of his tent; he will set me high on a rock.

Now my head is lifted up above my enemies all around me, and I will offer in his tent sacrifices with shouts of joy; I will sing and make melody to the Lord.

Hear, O Lord, when I cry aloud, be gracious to me and answer me!

"Come," my heart says, "seek his face!" Your face, Lord, do I seek.

Do not hide your face from me. Do not turn your servant away in anger, you who have been my help. Do not cast me off, do not forsake me, O God of my salvation!

If my father and mother forsake me, the Lord will take me up.

Teach me your way, O Lord, and lead me on a level path because of my enemies.

Do not give me up to the will of my adversaries, for false witnesses have risen against me, and they are breathing out violence.

I believe that I shall see the goodness of the Lord in the land of the living.

Wait for the Lord; be strong, and let your heart take courage; wait for the Lord!

I chose Psalm 27, verses I have memorized, simply because these are the verses, I often read to other people who are faced with troubling life situations. "The Lord is the strength of my life; of what shall I be afraid? Be strong and take courage and always wait for the Lord." I have often used the Philippians passage to remind people, as well as myself, that the Apostle Paul used the words here, "I have learned to be content" and "I have learned that I can all things through Christ who strengthens me." Paul is saying here that it took some time for him to learn those two important lessons of life—it didn't happen overnight. It took time and it took a number of life experiences for Paul to learn to be content and to learn that he could in fact accomplish very challenging and difficult tasks through Christ who strengthened him.

Let me just add, if I may, that I am still in the process of learning these things. Every time I see someone, or think of someone I might help, over the years I have become even more conscious of what Jesus said, "When you do it unto the least of them, you do it unto me." It would have been very easy at those times for me to just pass them by or to do something else. I have tried in the years of my ministry to be more conscious of those people who are the "least of them around me." And you know, when you consciously look for these people, they are all around you.

Romans 8:28
And we know that in all things God works for the good of those who love him, who have been called according to his purpose.

After all the messes I have made in my life, I have always tried to remember the Romans 8:28 passage. It is one of my favorites—"that God works for good" (that is, His good) "in all things." I like to say to people that God is indeed able to work His good out of my goofs if I but only turn to Him and let Him do His good.

Ephesians 2:8-9

For it is by grace you have been saved, through faith—and this is not from yourselves, it is the gift of God—not by works, so that no one can boast.

All, I can say about the Ephesians 3:8-9 passage is that this is one of my favorite theological passages. In fact, whenever I encounter a person who expresses to me that they are relying on their own goodness to get into Heaven, I will often share with them what the Bible says about this, "Salvation is not of your own doing, it is the gift of God."

Matthew 6:25-34

"Therefore I tell you, do not worry about your life, what you will eat or drink; or about your body, what you will wear. Is not life more than food, and the body more than clothes? Look at the birds of the air; they do not sow or reap or store away in barns, and yet your heavenly Father feeds them. Are you not much more valuable than they? Can any one of you by worrying add a single hour to your life?

"And why do you worry about clothes? See how the flowers of the field grow. They do not labor or spin. Yet I tell you

that not even Solomon in all his splendor was dressed like one of these. If that is how God clothes the grass of the field, which is here today and tomorrow is thrown into the fire, will he not much more clothe you—you of little faith? So do not worry, saying, 'What shall we eat?' or 'What shall we drink?' or 'What shall we wear?' For the pagans run after all these things, and your heavenly Father knows that you need them. But seek first his kingdom and his righteousness, and all these things will be given to you as well. Therefore do not worry about tomorrow, for tomorrow will worry about itself. Each day has enough trouble of its own.

Of course, the very last passage, the one from Matthew 6 in my estimation is all about trusting God to take care of us even when the worries and the troubles of our lives seem to be overtaking us. Now I am sure you have had your share of worries and troubles and I have had mine. But I can honestly say that over the years I have learned to trust the Lord to indeed give me just enough light to take my next step. It has taken nearly 80 years to learn this, but I think I have.

I would be remiss if I didn't say to you all how deeply indebted, I am to you all for giving me the opportunity to close out my nearly 55 years of pastoral ministry at this church, a church which I dearly love with all my heart. That is one of the reasons why Liz and I are not leaving you. You're going to have to put up with us. In fact, Liz has said that some Sunday you may actually find us sitting in your usual seat.

Finally, for those of you who feel this is an ending of something good, let me just challenge you to think of it instead as a beginning and not an ending. It is the beginning of a new era for Trinity Lutheran Church. Don't forget my friends that Liz and I are going to be here to experience with you what God has in store for our congregation in the years ahead. I want you to know that Liz and I indeed trust God to work His good in this congregation in the years ahead. Our question to you is, "Do you trust Him to do this?"

Amen.

Appendix

Pastor to Host Negro Child Despite Threats

SOUTH HAVEN — Despite threats, a Lutheran church minister remains undeterred in his plan to bring a Negro child here for two-week stay later this month.

Seeking protection, if necessary, the Rev. Roger L. Thompson, pastor of Our Saviour Lutheran Church, conferred Monday with Porter County Sheriff Myrick (Mike) Crampton.

According to Thompson, one agitator has threatened to "bomb" the family's home at 39 Clear Creek Drive, while another apparently intends to burn a "cross" on the lawn.

The minister said these came as "second - hand threats," related to him by members of his congregation as they heard it told.

Thompson told The Post-Tribune he has no idea of the identity of the persons threatening these reprisals.

The minister's proposed participation in the program was announced to his church congregation on Sunday, June 4.

His part in the rural summer vacation program — a nation-wide church project — "is a personal endeavor," and isn't necessarily sanctioned by his congregation.

The agreement calls for a Negro boy — 7 to 9 years of age — from an impoverished area of Chicago to live with the Thompsons from June 24 through July 8.

The program isn't new to Porter County.

Such a venture, under sponsorship of Immanuel Lutheran Church, is currently under way in Valparaiso, according to Thompson.

"It is not my intent to force integration in South Haven," he said. Rather, "I'm doing this merely to help a child — as any Christian would do."

He pictured the Negro child's opportunity to see "the better side of life" as a mutual education for all parties.

The pastor said the reaction in this community hasn't been all negative, however.

He said he's been approached by at least three other families who have expressed a desire to have the boy visit their homes here.

Thompson stressed the child will visit other South Haven families "by invitation only."

Regarding the threats, Thompson commented "They're trying to tell me who I can have in my home, which I consider an invasion of my own rights."

"This is what infuriates me the most."

The threats, he claims, are consequential to every resident of South Haven, since they are "implied infringements" upon the rights of the entire community.

Negro Boy To Visit In Home

A South Haven minister has issued a statement explaining his position concerning a future visit in his home of a Chicago Negro youth, after he said he received threats on his life.

The Rev. Roger L. Thompson of Our Savior Lutheran church told The V-M he received threats of bodily harm, cross burnings and the possibility of a bomb being placed in his home when residents learned he and his family would have a Negro youth as guest in their home this summer.

"I am not a civil rightist," he explained. "I am doing this because I want to help a little boy who needs this kind of opportunity. I am simply doing what any Christian would consider doing.

Not Proving Point

"I am not doing this to force integration, nor simply to prove a point, nor to stir up trouble."

The Rev. Thompson made a report of the threats Monday to the Porter County Sheriff's department.

The youth's visit under the sponsorship of the Rural Summer Vacation program is a project of the Lutheran Human Relations association of America. The youngster, 7 to 9 years old, will spend two weeks in the Thompson home, June 24 to July 8.

Denying Basic Right

The Rev. Thompson said he made the statement because he felt people did not understand his reason for becoming involved in the program. He said he felt people were concerned he was pushing integration.

"By threatening me and trying to tell me who may visit in my home they are denying me the basic right I have and this very threat actually threatens the rights of other people to decide who will visit in their homes," the Rev. Thompson said.

Made in the USA
Lexington, KY
20 February 2019